OECD *Economic Surveys*
Electronic Books

The OECD, recognising the strategic role of electronic publishing, will be issuing the OECD *Economic Surveys*, both for the Member countries and for countries of Central and Eastern Europe covered by the Organisation's Centre for Co-operation with Economies in Transition, as electronic books with effect from the 1994/1995 series -- incorporating the text, tables and figures of the printed version. The information will appear on screen in an identical format, including the use of colour in graphs.

The electronic book, which retains the quality and readability of the printed version throughout, will enable readers to take advantage of the new tools that the ACROBAT software (included on the diskette) provides by offering the following benefits:

❑ User-friendly and intuitive interface
❑ Comprehensive index for rapid text retrieval, including a table of contents, as well as a list of numbered tables and figures
❑ Rapid browse and search facilities
❑ Zoom facility for magnifying graphics or for increasing page size for easy readability
❑ Cut and paste capabilities
❑ Printing facility
❑ Reduced volume for easy filing/portability

Working environment: DOS, Windows or Macintosh.

Subscription: FF 1 800   US$317   £200   DM 545

Single issue: FF 130   US$24   £14   DM 40

Complete 1994/1995 series on CD-ROM:

FF 2 000   US$365   £220   DM 600

Please send your order to OECD Electronic Editions or, preferably, to the Centre or bookshop with whom you placed your initial order for this Economic Survey.

OECD
ECONOMIC
SURVEYS

1994-1995

FRANCE

ORGANISATION FOR ECONOMIC CO-OPERATION AND DEVELOPMENT

ORGANISATION FOR ECONOMIC CO-OPERATION AND DEVELOPMENT

Pursuant to Article 1 of the Convention signed in Paris on 14th December 1960, and which came into force on 30th September 1961, the Organisation for Economic Co-operation and Development (OECD) shall promote policies designed:

— to achieve the highest sustainable economic growth and employment and a rising standard of living in Member countries, while maintaining financial stability, and thus to contribute to the development of the world economy;

— to contribute to sound economic expansion in Member as well as non-member countries in the process of economic development; and

— to contribute to the expansion of world trade on a multilateral, non-discriminatory basis in accordance with international obligations.

The original Member countries of the OECD are Austria, Belgium, Canada, Denmark, France, Germany, Greece, Iceland, Ireland, Italy, Luxembourg, the Netherlands, Norway, Portugal, Spain, Sweden, Switzerland, Turkey, the United Kingdom and the United States. The following countries became Members subsequently through accession at the dates indicated hereafter: Japan (28th April 1964), Finland (28th January 1969), Australia (7th June 1971), New Zealand (29th May 1973) and Mexico (18th May 1994). The Commission of the European Communities takes part in the work of the OECD (Article 13 of the OECD Convention).

Publié également en français.

3 2280 00481 3481

Table of contents

Boxes

Tables

Figures

BASIC STATISTICS OF FRANCE (1994)

THE LAND

Area (1000 sq. km)	549.1	Major cities (inhabitants), 1990:	
Agricultural area (1000 sq. km), 1993	302.2	Paris	2 152 423
		Marseille	800 550
		Lyon	415 487

THE PEOPLE

Population (thousands), 1.1.1994	57 804	Total labour force (thousands)	25 530
Number of inhabitants per sq. km	105		
Total increase in population (thousands)	274		

PRODUCTION

Gross domestic product at market prices		Origin of the gross domestic product, at market	
(billion FF)	7 376.9	prices:	
Gross domestic product per head (US $)	22 986	Agriculture	2.6
Gross fixed investment:		Industry	23.8
Per cent of GDP	18.3	Construction	4.9
Per head (US $)	4 198	Services	68.7
		Total	100

GENERAL GOVERNMENT
(ESNA concept)

Current expenditure (% of GDP)	51.0
Current revenue (% of GDP)	48.8
Current fixed investment (% of GDP)	3.4

FOREIGN TRADE

Exports of goods and services (% of GDP)	22.8	Imports of goods and services (% of GDP)	20.6
Main exports as a percentage of total exports (SITC), 1993:		Main imports as a percentage of total imports (SITC), 1993:	
Food, beverages and tobacco (0 + 1)	15.5	Food, beverages and tobacco (0 + 1)	10.7
Machinery and transport equipment (7)	38.4	Machinery and transport equipment (7)	34.5
Iron and steel products (67 + 68)	5.2	Iron and steel products (67 + 68)	4.6
Chemical products (5)	14.2	Chemical products (5)	11.4
Textile products (65)	2.8	Mineral fuels, lubricants and related materials (3)	8.9

THE CURRENCY

Monetary unit: the franc	Currency units per US $, average of daily figures:	
	Year 1994	5.55
	June 1995	4.92

Note: An international comparison of certain basic statistics is given in an Annex table.

This Survey is based on the Secretariat's study prepared for the annual review of France by the Economic and Development Review Committee on 6 July 1995.

•

After revisions in the light of discussions during the review, final approval of the Survey for publication was given by the Committee on 27 July 1995 .

•

The previous Survey of France was issued in March 1994.

Introduction

Slow growth between 1990 and 1992 turned into a recession in 1993. Weak activity was accompanied by a significant rise in unemployment and a slowdown in the growth of capital stock. At the time of the previous Survey of France 18 months ago it was thought that domestic demand would remain weak and activity in the rest of Europe subdued. However, the economy recovered strongly during 1994, due to a sharp turnaround in external demand and a strong contribution from stockbuilding, followed by a pick-up in domestic demand since mid-1994. By the end of 1994, growth had reached nearly 4 per cent (year-on-year). Private sector employment has responded faster than usual to the economic upswing and the unemployment rate has declined by ³/₄ percentage point, to 11.6 per cent. Owing to the considerable amount of cyclical slack, wage and price inflation has decelerated considerably since 1990, but the process of disinflation is probably over. While growth may have weakened in the first half of 1995, the demand outlook remains favourable. Investment seems poised to be very dynamic in 1995 and 1996, reflecting strong profitability and a narrowing output gap in industry. Private consumption may be bolstered by rising employment and GDP is likely to expand at a rate of around 3 per cent in 1995 and 1996, with inflation remaining under control. The unemployment rate could fall to around 11 per cent in 1996.

In the early 1990s, the government budget deficit rose, reaching 6 per cent of GDP in 1993, as a consequence of slow growth and, to a lesser extent, a rise in the structural government deficit. In order to redress the situation and to rein in the rapid debt accumulation, the Government presented a tight 1994 Budget and introduced structural measures to put the social security schemes on a sounder financial footing. Despite the reforms and slowing expenditure growth, the deficit of the social security system did not fall as much as expected. The growth of state outlays was much stronger than budgeted, but the deficit target of FF 300 billion was met. In summary, general government net borrowing was little changed from the 1993 level. The previous Government's Budget for 1995 aimed at keeping the lid on expenditure and reducing the deficit. Monetary policy eased considerably during 1994, but tightened again significantly in March 1995, following the franc's fall in the wake of international and ERM currency turbulence. While the franc is still trading at a relatively low rate against the Deutschemark, it has appreciated in effective terms.

The new Government outlined its programme in May 1995: its top priority is to reduce unemployment significantly by continuing to reduce indirect labour costs for the least qualified, and by introducing new employment programmes for the long-term unemployed and young people. On the other hand, the minimum wage was raised substantially in mid-1995. The Government also announced measures to boost residential construction and to lower costs for small and medium-sized enterprises. As far as macroeconomic policies are concerned, the new Government is committed to making the adjustments necessary to meet the Maastricht criteria in 1997.

Earlier structural reforms, such as the privatisation programme, the multi-annual labour market reform package, and changes to the health care system have been pursued over the last 18 months. Apart from the privatisation programme, the reform of goods and services markets has received little attention. However, some sectors, such as transport services, have been the subject of considerable policy and structural change over the last decade. The transport sector was heavily regulated until the mid-1980s, since then many access and pricing restrictions have been removed. Nonetheless, distortions remain and the Government continues to play an important role in providing infrastructure and supervising state-owned enterprises. Transport policies are reviewed in detail in the special chapter.

Chapter I of this Survey reviews recent developments and short-term prospects. Chapter II evaluates recent fiscal and monetary policies and includes a discussion of medium and long-term fiscal policy requirements. It also provides an overview of structural policy reforms, other than labour market policies, which are reviewed in more detail in Chapter III, and transport policies, which are the subject of Chapter IV. A summary of the key points of the Survey, together with policy considerations, is provided in the Conclusions.

I. Recent trends and short-term outlook

After experiencing a sharp recession in 1993, which was more marked than had been projected in the previous survey 18 months earlier (–1.5 per cent compared with an estimated –0.8 per cent), real GDP has recovered strongly, activity in the fourth quarter of 1994 was 3.7 per cent higher than a year earlier. The resumption of growth was driven initially by exports and a strong contribution from stockbuilding, and then, during the second half of the year, by a strengthening of final domestic demand. The recovery was particularly strong in industry, with activity returning to the level of the early 1990s.

Cyclical indicators point to some slowdown in activity in recent months, reflecting a lower growth contribution from stockbuilding, and probably also pre-electoral uncertainty and turbulence in foreign exchange markets. If external market growth remains strong, the slowdown should be only temporary. Indeed, the financial situation of companies is much more favourable than during previous recoveries, and as unused capacity is gradually absorbed, the growth of business investment is set to accelerate. The substantial pick-up in employment, which was stronger than in previous cycles, should provide the basis for a strengthening of household consumption. Lastly, despite the appreciation of the franc, wage restraint should make it possible to maintain satisfactory external competitiveness, so that exports should continue to grow briskly. Growth of GDP could reach some 3 per cent in both 1995 and 1996. Against this background, inflation should rise only a little, despite the price level effect of the VAT rate increase, while the current balance should continue to show a substantial surplus. Unemployment should continue to fall, reaching 11 per cent of the labour force in 1996.

Demand and output

Up to mid-1994, the recovery, which got under way in the second quarter of 1993, was based primarily on exports and a substantial slowdown in de-stocking

(Table 1). Export markets picked up strongly, growing by 6 per cent in the second half of 1993 and by over 10 per cent in 1994, a rate not seen since 1988. Rapid export growth had a very favourable impact on the business climate, even though the foreign trade balance did not contribute – *ex post* – to growth, since the recovery of foreign sales was accompanied by a parallel rise in imports. The rapid growth of international trade led to a reversal in demand expectations, prompting renewed stockbuilding. Whereas the running down of inventories had weighed heavily on growth from mid-1992, they began to rise again gradually from mid-1994, contributing nearly half of the growth observed in 1994. However, inventory levels in industry are still considered to be relatively low, particularly for intermediate goods, so that the rebuilding of inventories should continue.

On the other hand, the recovery of business investment so far has been fairly limited compared with previous cycles. While rising during 1994, the level of business investment on average remained virtually unchanged and even fell in

Table 1. **The cycle in the 1990s**

Annual growth rates at 1980 prices

	Downward phase			Upward phase	
	1991	1992	1993	1994	1995 I
Private consumption	1.4	1.4	0.2	1.5	1.6
Public consumption	2.8	3.4	3.3	1.0	1.8
Fixed investment	0	–3.1	–5.8	1.4	4.7
General government	5.4	4.0	–0.3	3.3	2.5
Households	–4.1	–4.2	–6.7	2.5	0.3
Business	0.4	–4.7	–7.1	0.3	7.4
Final domestic demand	1.3	0.8	–0.5	1.4	2.3
Stockbuilding[1]	–0.7	–0.4	–1.8	1.6	–0.1
Total domestic demand	0.6	0.4	–2.3	3.0	2.2
Exports	4.1	4.9	–0.4	5.8	7.8
Imports	3.1	1.1	–3.4	6.6	6.5
Foreign balance[1]	0.2	1.0	0.8	–0.2	0.3
GDP	0.8	1.4	–1.5	2.8	2.6
Memorandum items:					
GDP:					
EU	3.3	1.0	–0.4	2.7	3.1
OECD	1.7	1.6	1.3	2.9	2.5

1. Contribution of change in stockbuilding and the external balance to GDP growth.
Source: OECD, *National Accounts* and estimates.

industry, and the investment ratio continued to fall, almost to the low point of 1984 (Figure 1). This is all the more striking as the current financial situation of companies is exceptionally favourable compared with previous recoveries. With the acceleration of growth, continuing wage restraint and the sharp fall in financial costs, company profitability improved markedly in 1994, so that the self-financing ratio attained the very high level of 115 per cent (Table 2). Large companies saw a much greater improvement in their operating results and cash positions than did small and medium-sized enterprises. Being more exposed to foreign trade, large companies seem to have benefited substantially from the European recovery. Profitability (the difference between the business sector rate of return and interest rates) in general should no longer be a constraint on investment: it had worsened sharply up to the beginning of 1993 because of the rise in interest rates, but improved thereafter and, overall, it has probably stabilised recently, although still at levels below those of the late 1980s. Surveys also indicate that businesses no longer consider borrowing conditions to be an obstacle to investment.

Up to now investment has remained lower than traditional mechanisms explaining investment behaviour, such as the accelerator, profitability or financial variables, would have predicted. Instead of investing, businesses have sought to utilise their existing capacity more efficiently, by reorganising work methods and using temporary and fixed-term contracts. This rationalisation – and the scale of the recession – probably explains why the capacity utilisation rate in industry has risen only moderately, returning to the long-term average, despite buoyant demand. Furthermore, investment by major public enterprises has been scaled down following the completion of large programmes and this has impacted on overall capital formation. After the fall in investment since 1990 (more than 10 per cent up to 1994), the growth of capital stock slackened considerably, bearing down on potential output. With rising rates of capacity utilisation, businesses should speed up their capital expenditure. A strong recovery in business investment started in the second half of 1994, and business surveys show that projected investment in industry for 1995 is up by 13 per cent in value and that capital goods production and wholesale orders are still rising.

Residential investment was more buoyant in 1994, after having fallen by more than 15 per cent over the previous three years. Demand was bolstered by the fall in interest rates between early 1993 and mid-1994 and the programme of

Figure 1. **BUSINESS INVESTMENT:
AN INTERNATIONAL COMPARISON**

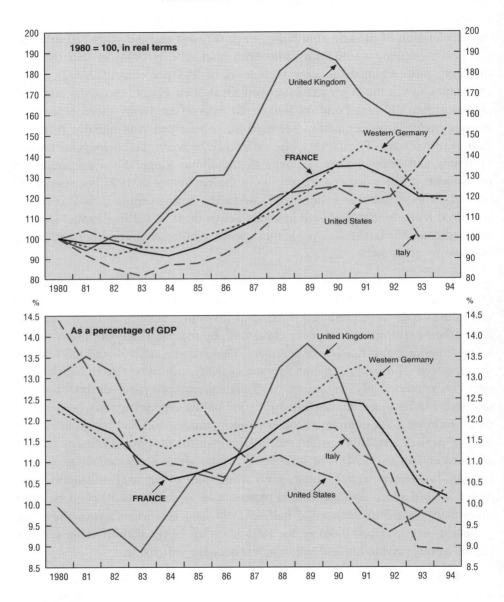

Source: OECD.

Table 2. **Saving, investment and net lending**

Per cent of GDP

	National (1 + 2)	Government (1)	Private (2)		
			Total	Business	Households
Saving					
Average 1970-80	25.7	3.7	22.1	8.4	13.7
Average 1981-90	20.2	1.3	18.9	9.0	9.9
1991	21.0	1.4	19.6	10.4	9.2
1992	19.9	−0.5	20.5	10.8	9.7
1993	18.1	−2.6	20.7	10.8	9.9
1994	19.0	−2.1	21.1	11.5	9.6
Investment [1]					
Average 1970-80	25.4	3.4	21.9	14.3	7.6
Average 1981-90	20.7	3.2	17.6	11.6	6.0
1991	21.5	3.5	18.0	12.5	5.5
1992	19.8	3.5	16.3	11.1	5.2
1993	17.1	3.2	13.9	9.1	4.8
1994	17.9	3.4	14.5	9.7	4.8
Net lending					
Average 1970-80	0.2	−0.4	0.6	−3.7	4.3
Average 1981-90	−0.6	−2.3	1.6	−1.4	3.0
1991	−0.6	−2.2	1.6	−1.9	3.5
1992	0.1	−4.0	4.2	−0.3	4.5
1993	1.0	−6.1	7.1	2.6	4.5
1994	0.7	−6.0	6.6	2.6	4.0

1. Fixed investment and stockbuilding.
Source: INSEE.

support for the housing sector which was adopted in mid-1993. This consisted essentially of increased aid for the construction of social housing, with an increase of 22 per cent over the initial budget. As the effects of this programme wore off, and borrowing terms became tighter, the market turned down again. Surveys indicate that demand has weakened, new private housing prices are still falling, and that the stock of unsold dwellings has begun to rise rapidly again since the end of 1994.

Although recent surveys show a considerable improvement in consumer sentiment, private consumption was still hesitant at the beginning of 1995, after accelerating in the second half of 1994. Purchases of durable goods were boosted in 1994 by government subsidies for car purchases. According to the manufactur-

7

ers, these subsidies probably accounted for 450 000 new registrations in 1994, whereas the average long-term replacement rate for vehicles over 10 years old is some 220 000. However, the rate of increase in the number of new registrations has slowed in recent months, and household consumption of manufactured products has been flat since the autumn of 1994. Household real disposable income picked up gradually, after having stagnated in 1993 owing to job cuts and the rise in income tax and social security contributions (Table 3). In 1994 the pick-up in employment more than offset wage restraint and the curb on transfer income resulting from the reform of the unemployment insurance system and measures in the health sector. Nonetheless, despite the improvement in the labour market, households did not appreciably modify their propensity to save and, after having fallen slightly between mid-1993 and the second quarter of 1994, the savings ratio picked up again in the second half of the year. Overall, while the recent changes in the savings ratio are in line with its main determinants – income and inflation – its level is still considerably higher than past relationships would suggest. According to recent work by the OECD, this phenomenon could be explained by a greater interest-rate sensitivity on the part of households, with substitution effects outweighing income effects.

Table 3. **Household appropriation account**

Percentage changes

	1991	1992	1993	1994
Compensation of employees	4.8	3.8	1.5	2.5
Property and entrepreneurial income	6.5	4.2	0.3	2.8
Current transfers received	6.9	6.2	6.1	3.1
Total income	5.9	4.4	2.6	3.1
Less:				
Direct taxes	17.6	4.2	4.1	5.8
Current transfers paid	4.2	4.7	2.3	2.7
Disposable income	5.4	4.4	2.6	2.9
Private consumption	4.6	3.8	2.4	3.3
Real disposable income	2.1	2.0	0.3	1.1
Saving rate	13.2	13.7	13.8	13.5
Financial saving rate	4.9	6.2	6.1	5.4

Source: OECD, *National Accounts.*

Employment, wage and price inflation

After falling substantially between 1991 and 1993, employment staged a recovery during 1994 (Table 4). The employment response to the economic upturn came earlier than during previous recoveries and was also stronger. Job creation was also considerably more dynamic than in the European Union as a whole in 1994, even though output growth was broadly the same. In the year to March 1995, the number of employees in the private sector grew by 1¾ per cent, with a 3 per cent growth of jobs in the service sector,[1] while the decline in manufacturing employment came to a halt. Many new jobs were in part-time work and in employment with temporary job agencies, both providing greater flexibility and, in the case of part-time work, lower costs due to government incentives. Moreover, the incidence of short-time work fell steeply.

Since the early 1990s, overall employment developments have not deviated much from those in the private sector, as a fast rise in government employment more than offset the trend decline in the number of self-employed. The rise in government employment partly reflects the rapid expansion of employment programmes (*contrats emploi-solidarité*). In 1994, the number of people in these programmes rose further, even though their estimated contribution to employment growth was minor in 1994. By early 1995 overall employment was still

Table 4. **Employment and productivity**

Percentage changes

	1990	1991	1992	1993	1994
Labour force	0.5	0.6	0.4	0.3	1.2
Unemployment rate	8.9	9.4	10.4	11.7	12.3
Total employment	1.0	0.0	−0.7	−1.2	0.5
Employees	1.5	0.3	−0.2	−0.9	0.9
Private sector	1.9	0.1	−0.9	−2.2	0.7
Government	0.2	1.0	1.7	2.8	1.4
Self-employed	−2.0	−2.4	−3.5	−3.4	−2.4
Labour productivity					
Output per employed person	1.5	0.8	2.0	−0.3	2.3
Hourly productivity	2.2	1.1	2.5	1.1	2.6

Source: INSEE and OECD.

1 per cent below the 1990 level, although labour productivity growth showed a cyclical slow-down below its trend growth rate of 2 to 2¼ per cent between 1990 and 1993. Private sector hourly productivity growth (adjusting for part-timers, overtime and short-time) slowed by less than overall output per employed person.

The job situation has improved considerably and the unemployment rate has fallen by ¾ percentage point since its peak in the second quarter of 1994, and stood at 11.6 per cent in May 1995. While the steep rise in unemployment between 1990 and 1993 had been cushioned by a slow-down in labour force growth, discouraged workers flowed back into the labour market in 1994. According to OECD estimates, the rise in unemployment since the early 1990s is largely cyclical, the structural component having remained stable at about 9 per cent since the late 1980s. Labour market developments and policies are discussed in greater detail in Chapter III.

The rising amount of slack in goods and labour markets lowered overall inflation from close to 3 per cent in 1990 to 1½ per cent in 1994 (Table 5). Wage inflation declined by more than price inflation: increases in private sector wages per employee fell from more than 5 per cent in 1990 to just above 1 per cent in 1994. This is among the lowest rates in the OECD area and has contributed to robust job creation since mid-1993. On an hourly basis the deceleration was less marked (a 1.9 per cent rise in 1994), largely reflecting the fast rise in part-time work.[2] The deceleration in wage increases led to a fall in real wages per employee in 1993 and 1994, after very slow growth in 1991 and 1992, and real labour costs – which had risen by 0.6 per cent on average between 1990 and 1994 – increased much less rapidly than underlying productivity growth (2.2 per cent). These developments are in line with the predictions of the OECD's private sector wage equation and corroborate the view that structural unemployment has not risen further since the late 1980s.

Low cost pressure and cyclical slack reduced consumer price inflation to 1.7 per cent in 1994, the lowest rate since 1956. In recent months, the prices of manufactured goods have started to rise somewhat faster, from a very low rate, while disinflation in the private services component has continued. Rates of inflation of close to 2 per cent or even below, which have prevailed since 1992, are among the lowest in the OECD area, and underlying inflation[3] has been close to 1 per cent in recent months. Producer price inflation has been close to 1 per cent since 1992, although it accelerated somewhat recently.[4]

Table 5. **Wage and price inflation**

Percentage changes

	1990	1991	1992	1993	1994
Wage developments					
Private sector					
Hourly wage rate	5.4	4.8	4.0	2.0	1.9
Wage sum per employee	5.2	4.6	3.6	2.1	1.1
Compensation per employee	5.1	4.5	4.0	2.2	1.1
Real labour cost	1.9	1.1	1.8	−0.3	−0.3
Unit labour cost	4.2	3.8	1.7	2.1	−1.2
Total economy					
Compensation per employee	5.1	4.4	4.1	2.4	1.6
Unit labour cost	4.0	4.0	2.4	3.0	−0.3
Price and cost developments					
Private consumption deflator	2.9	3.2	2.4	2.2	1.8
GDP deflator	3.1	3.3	2.1	2.5	1.3
Producer prices, non financial enterprises	2.4	2.2	0.9	0.8	1.2
Unit cost	2.5	2.1	0.9	0.9	0.4
Contribution of:					
Intermediate consumption	0.6	0.9	−0.2	−0.1	1.0
Capital cost	0.4	0.0	0.4	0.0	−0.7
Taxes	0.2	0.1	0.1	0.4	0.3
Labour cost	1.3	1.2	0.6	0.5	−0.2
Memorandum items:					
Profit share	35.6	35.7	35.8	35.3	35.8
Output gap, business sector [1]	1.5	−0.2	−1.2	−4.9	−4.0
Capacity utilisation in manufacturing [2]	88.1	85.2	83.4	80.5	82.4

1. OECD measure, based on production function.
2. INSEE measure, based on business surveys.
Source: INSEE and OECD.

In view of the large amount of cyclical slack, it is surprising that the process of disinflation has not gone further since 1992 and that profit margins have remained at such high levels. An *ex post* simulation of the wage-price block of OECD's INTERLINK model suggests that on the basis of past relationships inflation should indeed have dropped further, to close to zero in 1994.[5] Several hypotheses[6] may explain why the process of disinflation has stopped, even though their quantitative importance is difficult to pin down:

- Official measures of inflation may exaggerate price rises. INSEE's data gathering may rely largely on list prices, so that the multiplication of sales promotions and discount sales in recent years may bias the official inflation and profit estimates upwards. In the United States and Canada, hedonic price indices are used to estimate quality improvements for electronic equipment. This reduces inflation rates considerably, even at the aggregate level. After these adjustments, measured rates of inflation are still thought to contain an upward bias.

- The effect of output gaps on profit margins may not be symmetric over the business cycle. Slack in goods markets may not reduce inflation by as much as a positive output gap raises it. Turner (1995) finds such an asymmetric effect for most G7 countries, including France.
- The user cost of capital may play a larger role in price setting, especially if many liquidity-constrained firms face high short-term interest rates for a prolonged period.
- The sharp fall in industrial investment reduced capital stock growth in this sector to $1/2$ to 1 per cent in 1994 and, according to INSEE's estimate of potential output (based on business surveys), capacity utilisation in the manufacturing sector has already recovered to close to its long-term average. However, output gaps are difficult to estimate with any precision. INSEE, for instance, also notes that capacity utilisation has risen much less than output, as utilisation of existing equipment has been extended considerably. The output gap could also be smaller than suggested by the OECD's estimate of potential output (based on a production function for the business sector).

The balance of payments

The current account surplus (0.7 per cent of GDP) remained substantial during a phase of strong recovery, attesting to the high level of external and domestic competitiveness, despite the effective appreciation of the franc. Indeed, wage restraint was more marked than in the main partner countries and relative unit labour costs in a common currency stabilised (Figure 2). With widening margins, relative export prices have risen somewhat since 1991, but non-price competitiveness, as indicated by French capital accumulation relative to its competitors, improved. Thus, exporters have broadly maintained their market shares. At the same time, the merchandise import penetration ratio fell slightly. Overall, the trade surplus continued to widen owing to the increased positive balance on

Figure 2. **EXTERNAL COMPETITIVENESS**[1]

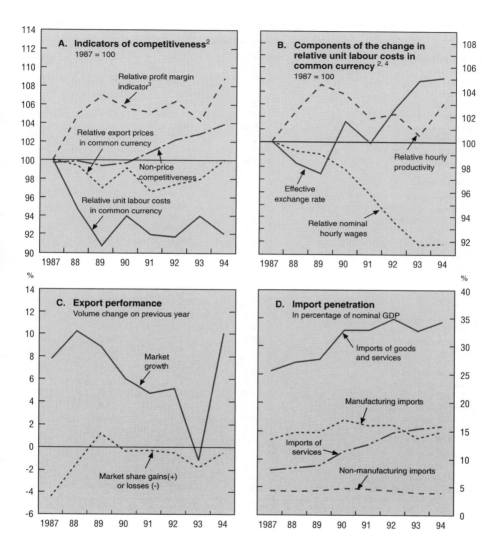

A. Indicators of competitiveness[2]
1987 = 100

Relative profit margin indicator[3]

Relative export prices in common currency

Non-price competitiveness

Relative unit labour costs in common currency

B. Components of the change in relative unit labour costs in common currency [2, 4]
1987 = 100

Relative hourly productivity

Effective exchange rate

Relative nominal hourly wages

C. Export performance
Volume change on previous year

Market growth

Market share gains(+) or losses (-)

D. Import penetration
In percentage of nominal GDP

Imports of goods and services

Manufacturing imports

Imports of services

Non-manufacturing imports

1. 1994 figures are OECD estimates.
2. In manufacturing. A rise in the price curves or relative costs denotes a loss of competitiveness. Non price competitiveness is measured as the smoothed ratio of capital accumulation in France and in eight major partner countries.
3. Export prices/relative labour costs in manufacturing.
4. Only 16 competitors were taken into account.
Source: OECD.

Table 6. **Balance of payments**

Balances, FF billion

	1991	1992	1993	1994
Current balance	−34.5	20.5	52.4	54.4
Goods	−49.8	15.3	42.6	53.8
Services	17.6	12.3	14.1	16.3
of which:				
Tourism	51.0	59.7	60.7	60.5
Factor income	−32.6	−48.3	−47.9	−54.9
Other goods and services	39.0	40.1	30.3	29.1
Unilateral transfers	−41.4	−47.1	−34.6	−44.8
Private	−14.4	−17.0	−3.9	−4.6
Official	−26.9	−30.1	−30.7	−40.2
Capital transfers	−3.2	2.1	−0.5	−25.5
Long-term capital	12.4	117.9	−23.7	−243.0
Trade credits	3.6	0.6	11.9	−2.5
Direct investment	−53.2	−16.8	−0.1	−1.2
Outward	−115.6	−101.1	−68.9	−59.5
Inward	62.5	84.3	68.8	58.3
Public investment	−3.9	−3.5	−3.8	−3.6
Loans	−14.8	−49.5	−48.5	58.8
Private non-financial	−1.6	8.1	1.6	−0.2
Financial	11.1	−38.7	−35.8	48.4
Public	−24.3	−18.9	−14.4	10.7
Portfolio investment	80.6	187.1	16.9	−294.5
By residents	−84.2	−101.4	−176.0	−120.1
Non-residents	167.0	282.9	194.8	−169.0
Others	−2.2	5.5	−1.8	−5.5
Short-term capital [1]	0.0	−151.5	−43.3	237.5
Private non-financial	−35.5	−21.2	211.1	27.9
Banking	4.3	−240.3	−282.2	280.4
Public	31.2	109.9	27.8	−70.8
of which: Official reserves	29.9	−13.0	30.9	−13.5
Errors and omissions	25.4	11.0	15.0	−23.5
Memorandum items:				
Basic balance [2]	−25.3	140.5	28.2	−214.1
Overall balance [3]	−60.8	130.3	254.3	−209.7
Balance on official settlements [4]	−31.1	−110.0	−27.9	70.7

1. A + sign denotes a decrease in claims abroad or an increase in foreign liabilities. A − sign denotes an increase in claims abroad or a decrease in foreign liabilities.
2. Sum of balances on current and long-term capital accounts and on capital transfers.
3. Sum of the basic balance and the balance on short-term private non-financial capital transactions, and net errors and omissions.
4. Sum of overall balance and balance on short-term financial capital transactions of the banking sector.
Source: Banque de France and Ministère des Finances.

agro-food and manufacturing, the reduction in the energy deficit resulting from the depreciation of the dollar, and the mild weather. In contrast, the agricultural surplus narrowed sharply between 1993 and 1994 as a result of the reform of the Common Agricultural Policy (see Chapter II). The surplus on the tourism balance did not change much in 1994, despite an increase of 5.3 per cent in spending by residents abroad and the depreciation of the lira, peseta and escudo. The most recent indicators suggest that trade was still very buoyant at the beginning of 1995. The trade surplus continued to widen during the first quarter and the level of foreign orders is still high.

Capital movements showed a sharp acceleration in net long-term capital outflows. Against a background of strong turbulence in international financial markets, the balance on portfolio investment, which had already narrowed appreciably in 1993, was reversed in 1994 (Table 6). Purchases of foreign securities by residents continued, albeit at a slower rate, while non-residents sold French securities – essentially bonds (OAT) and Treasury bills (BTAN) – on a large scale. This movement was particularly marked during the first half of the year, in line with a general trend towards a ''renationalisation'' of investments. The sale of French securities by non-residents needs to be seen in relation to the scale of the purchases (over FF 1 100 billion) between 1989 and 1993, and in the context of the rise in bond yields (some 2.5 points between end-1993 and end-1994). On the other hand, large net repayments of franc-denominated loans by non-residents were recorded, causing large inflows of bank sector capital (net inflows of FF 280 billion in 1994 against net outflows of about the same size in 1993) and the balance on short-term capital movements was reversed. Also, with the unwinding of the foreign exchange crisis in July 1993, official short-term net assets[7] improved markedly in 1994, up by FF 70.8 billion. Official reserves increased by FF 13.5 billion, while at the same time liabilities *vis-à-vis* non-residents, especially those denominated in French francs, fell by FF 59 billion.

The outlook to the end of 1996

Growth slowed somewhat in the first quarter of 1995, largely reflecting weak sales of consumer durables. On the other hand, business surveys remain optimistic. While the year started with a high level of expectation which declined in the months until April, order books remain solid, the production outlook stable at a high level, and inventories are still judged to be low in manufacturing. Prospects for investment are favourable (up by 13 per cent in nominal terms in industry) and consumer confidence has improved. Lastly, the international environment is set to remain buoyant, with export markets projected to grow by 7½ to 8 per cent throughout the forecast period.

The forecasts are based on policies in the Budget amendments voted in July 1995, and in particular on the assumption of unchanged taxation and an effort to reduce the public deficit through a curtailment of general government expenditure in 1996. After the period of electoral uncertainty, the pressures on the French franc have eased. The OECD's forecast is based on the assumption that short-term interest rates will fall significantly from June 1995, but they could rise in 1996 in line with German rates. On the other hand, long-term rates are projected to fall in this scenario.

In this context, activity should grow at a steady rate – some 3 per cent – mainly led by business demand (Table 7). Business investment is set to increase briskly due to high profit levels, the gradual taking-up of spare capacity, and the favourable outlook for demand. Lower long-term interest rates should also bolster business investment. The growth rate of capital stock could thus pick up to 2½ per cent in 1996, after having slowed since 1990 (from 3¼ per cent to under 2 per cent in 1994). Stockbuilding could continue to rise, from the low levels of early 1995. However, its contribution to growth should lessen during the projection period. Household demand has remained fairly hesitant so far, but as employment rises, the growth of real disposable income will strengthen in 1995, but slow again in 1996 due to the effects of the direct and indirect tax increases, and households should reduce their precautionary saving. Despite high interest rates on housing loans, private residential construction could recover in 1996, partly reflecting recent government measures.

Domestic demand could grow at a rate of some 3 to 3¼ per cent, in line with the projected European average. The contribution of external trade to growth could be slightly negative, even though favourable competitiveness should enable exporters to maintain their market shares. With GDP growth of 3 per cent, job creation should remain robust, and the unemployment rate continue to come down, to 11 per cent in 1996. The rate of inflation could rise to 2½ per cent in the first half of 1996, reflecting the VAT rate increase, but might fall back in the second half due to the reduction in indirect labour costs. The improved labour-

Table 7. **Short-term projections**

Percentage changes, seasonally adjusted annual rates, 1980 prices

	1994	1995	1996	1995 I	1995 II	1996 I	1996 II
Private consumption	1.5	2	3	1½	2¾	2¾	3
Government consumption	1.0	1½	1	1¾	1	1	1
Gross fixed investment	1.4	5¼	5½	4¾	5½	5½	5¼
General government	3.3	2¾	2	2½	1½	2	2
Households	2.5	2½	2	¼	1	2¼	2¾
Business	0.3	7½	8	7½	9	8	7¼
Stockbuilding [1]	1.6	¼	0	0	¼	0	0
Total domestic demand	3.0	2¾	3¼	2¼	3	3	3¼
Exports of goods and services	5.8	7½	6¾	7¾	6¼	6¾	6¾
Imports of goods and services	6.6	6¾	7½	6½	7¾	7½	7½
Foreign balance [1]	–0.2	¼	–¼	¼	–½	–¼	–¼
GDP	2.8	3	3	2½	2¾	3	3
Employment	0.5	1¼	1	1½	1	1	1
Unemployment rate [2]	12.3	11½	11	11¾	11½	11	10¾
Household saving ratio [3]	13.5	13¾	13¼	..	..	..	..
Private consumption deflator	1.8	2	2½	1¾	2½	2½	2
GDP price deflator	1.5	2	2¼	2	2½	2¼	2¼
Short-term interest rates	5.8	6¼	5¼	7	5½	5¼	5½
Long-term interest rates	7.5	7¾	7¼	8	7½	7¼	7¼
General-government borrowing requirement [4]	–6.0	–5	–4½	..	..	..	..
Current balance [5]	0.7	1	¾	1	1	¾	¾

1. Contribution of change in stockbuilding and the foreign balance to GDP growth.
2. Per cent of the labour force.
3. Per cent of disposable income.
4. Per cent of GDP.
5. Per cent of GDP, including capital transfers.

Source: OECD.

market situation is likely to be accompanied by an acceleration in real wage increases, which would, however, be gradual given the still high level of unemployment. While the disinflation process is probably over, pressures on prices should remain weak. Spare capacity is likely to be taken up only slowly, and the rise in raw material prices to be offset by trimming margins. Despite the buoyant growth of domestic demand, the surplus on the current account should remain sizeable (¾ per of GDP on average) owing to a further improvement in the terms of trade.

The major risk to the projections concerns growth of investment. The recovery has become well established, but if activity slows, investment projects could be scaled back. In this respect, a major uncertainty is the impact of the recent marked exchange rate changes on major trading partners' economies and foreign demand could be lower than expected. In addition, the projections assume a rapid fall in short-term interest rates after the presidential elections. If they were to remain high, this would inevitably bear on domestic demand and on confidence, even though it is difficult to estimate the effect of high short-term interest rates on business investment and the saving ratio econometrically. However, as the level of the saving ratio has remained high during this recovery, consumption could grow more rapidly than projected. Inflation could be higher over the projection period, if margins do not react symmetrically to the increase in the VAT rate and the reduction in indirect labour costs. In addition, wages could adjust faster to the rise in the rate of inflation.

II.   Economic policies

Over the last 18 months, the macroeconomic policy setting has been geared towards attaining the Maastricht criteria by 1996, namely, cutting the sizeable government deficit and keeping internal and external currency stability. In addition, a reduction in the high level of unemployment has been a top priority. While inflation has remained low, exchange market tensions within the ERM have had to be fended off by raising short-term interest rates sharply, which has contained exchange rate volatility. The loosening of the ERM exchange rate bands in August 1993 and the independence of the Banque de France since 1994 have not changed monetary policy objectives. Progress in reducing the government deficit has been limited: for the State, expenditure rose much faster than foreseen in the medium-term fiscal plan and, despite a considerable reform effort in the social security schemes, their overall deficit changed little. At 6 per cent of GDP in 1994 (5.7 per cent if debt relief for the CFA[8] countries is excluded), general government net lending was unchanged from 1993. During 1994, most measures in the five-year labour market programme were implemented and the privatisation programme continued.

The new Government has announced its intention to make job creation its top priority. However, budget consolidation efforts will continue, even though it is now envisaged that the Maastricht deficit criterion will be realised only in 1997. Policy will focus on new labour market programmes, particularly for the long-term unemployed, the financing of which will rely largely on the increase in the VAT rate from 18.6 to 20.6 per cent. In addition, the minimum wage was raised by 4 per cent in July, double the rate applicable under the legal indexation mechanism.

Monetary policy

The Banque de France has been independent since 1994. It defines and implements monetary policy with the objective of maintaining price stability and it started to announce numerical inflation objectives in 1994. Decisions concerning the exchange rate regime and the parity of the franc remain with the Government, but implementation of policy is the responsibility of the Bank. The Government attaches great importance to achieving European Monetary Union at the earliest possible date, currently, the Maastricht targets for inflation and long-term interest rates are being met, and this performance is likely to continue until 1996.[9]

Interest rate and exchange rate developments

Since the exchange rate crisis in 1992, many currencies participating in the Exchange Rate Mechanism (ERM) have been subjected to recurrent speculative attacks, and the franc has been no exception. Since September 1992, exchange market tensions have occurred four times. Speculation was nourished by differences in macroeconomic policies across countries, for instance, differences in the pace of fiscal consolidation and divergent cyclical positions, which in the view of financial markets argued for a different policy setting. However, in the case of France foreign indebtedness is unlikely to have been a factor, as it is relatively low (Table 8).

Table 8. **Net foreign asset positions for selected OECD countries**

As a percentage of GDP

	1975	1985	1993
United States	4.1	1.0	−10.4
Japan	1.4	9.7	14.5
Germany	7.6	7.7	11.6
France	6.0[1]	−2.2	−3.1
Italy	−4.6	−7.6	−11.0
United Kingdom	1.9	21.9	3.8
Canada	−29.9	−35.6	−43.0
Netherlands	14.3[1]	24.0	13.0[2]
Spain	−6.4	−9.7	−16.8
Sweden	..	−20.8[3]	−46.4
Switzerland	..	111.8	102.1

1.   1980.
2.   1992.
3.   1989.
Source: OECD.

During the third speculative movement in July 1993, the Banque de France tightened monetary conditions by raising the short-term interest rate to 10 per cent (Figure 3). In order to contain exchange market tensions within the ERM, fluctuation bands were widened considerably – to 15 per cent. This was not seen as implying a change in monetary policies, but as a way of reducing the potential rewards to speculators. The monetary authorities reaffirmed that the central rate of the franc was in line with economic fundamentals.

This episode was followed by a cautious easing of monetary conditions – the Banque de France largely following market anticipation – while the franc recovered (Figure 4). In line with other ''hard core'' ERM countries, monetary easing continued during the first half of 1994: the repurchase rate was cut back to 6.4 per cent in May and the intervention rate to 5.0 per cent in July. The call money rate fell to 5.3 per cent in August, the differential against German rates remaining at below 50 basis points. The exchange rate fell somewhat against the Deutschemark between January and August 1994, while it strengthened in effective terms, mainly because of an appreciation against the dollar.

Rising tensions in international capital markets since the end of 1994 had little impact on the franc, even though it continued to decline slowly against the Deutschemark and short-term interest rates rose somewhat. However, in March 1995, international and ERM currency turbulence forced the franc down. At the low point, it reached 3.58 francs against the Deutschemark. In order to stabilise the franc, the repo rate was raised to 8 per cent. The franc recovered after the Bundesbank cut German rates, and the Banque de France lowered the repo rate in early April to 7³/₄ per cent. Currency tensions flared again during the first and second rounds of the presidential elections in late April and early May. The franc recovered thereafter and the repo rate was cut twice, to 7¹/₄ per cent in July. The franc is currently trading 3¹/₂ per cent below the strongest ERM currencies (FF 3.48 against the Deutschemark), but far above its lower band in the ERM grid. In effective terms the franc has appreciated in recent months, due to the weakness of the dollar, the lira and the peseta, and in June it stood 11 per cent above its 1991 level.

The events after mid-1992 show that it was difficult to contain volatility in exchange markets. While interest rates fell after these episodes and the franc recovered towards its central parity in the ERM, this came at the price of high real short-term interest rate differentials. The average real short-term interest rate

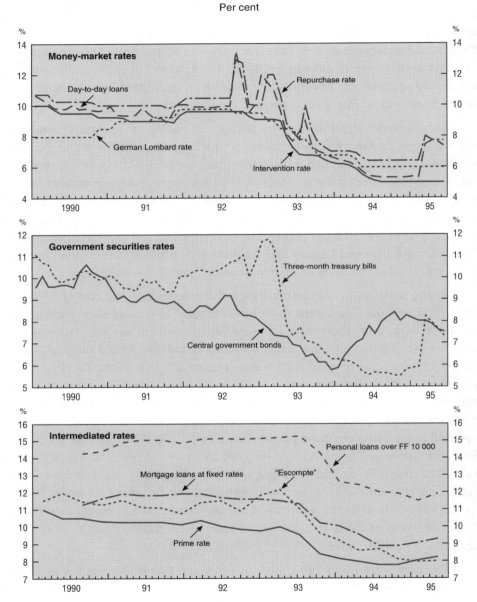

Figure 3. **INTEREST-RATE DEVELOPMENTS**

Per cent

Source: OECD.

Figure 4. **EXCHANGE RATES AND INTEREST-RATE DIFFERENTIALS**

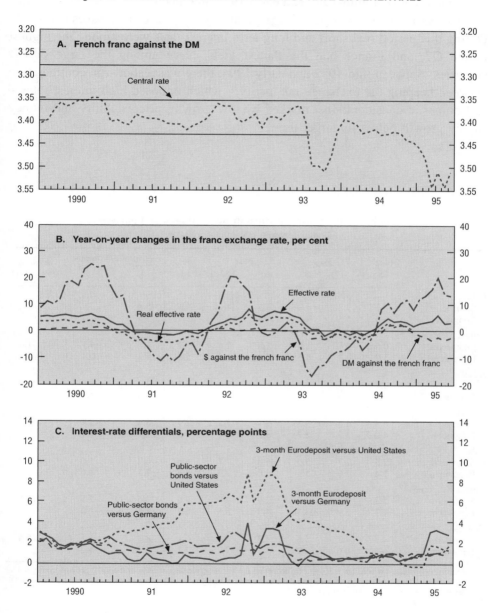

Source: OECD.

differential between mid-1992 and early 1995 amounted to 2½ percentage points against Germany and to 4 percentage points against the United States (Table 9). During this period real short and long-term interest rates were among the highest in the G7, and France had the flattest yield curve among the large OECD countries. Between mid-1992 and early 1994, there was a short-run contradiction between keeping the exchange rate parity – which imposed high interest rates – and domestic considerations, marked by low growth, price stability and money supply growth below its target limit.

Table 9. **Real interest rates in international comparison**

Nominal interest rates minus inflation [1]

	1992 S2	1993 S1	1993 S2	1994 S1	1994 S2	1995[2] S1	Average S2 92- S1 95	Differential against France	Exchange rate change[3]
France									
Short-term	8.7	7.3	4.8	4.5	4.2	5.1	5.8	..	8.2
Long-term	6.6	5.5	4.3	4.8	6.2	5.9	5.5	..	..
United States									
Short-term	0.5	0.6	1.0	1.8	2.6	3.7	1.7	–4.1	–1.0
Long-term	5.0	4.8	4.3	5.1	6.0	5.8	5.2	–0.4	..
Japan									
Short-term	2.4	2.5	1.7	1.3	2.9	2.7	2.3	–3.5	43.8
Long-term	3.8	3.6	3.1	3.5	4.2	3.7	3.6	–1.9	..
Germany									
Short-term	4.3	3.6	3.3	3.1	3.2	2.9	3.4	–2.4	11.7
Long-term	4.0	3.2	2.7	3.2	4.4	4.5	3.7	–1.9	..
Italy									
Short-term	12.3	7.7	5.0	5.0	4.7	5.5	6.7	1.0	–31.4
Long-term	9.4	7.9	5.1	5.0	7.3	8.1	7.1	1.6	..
United Kingdom									
Short-term	5.2	2.8	2.4	2.9	4.0	4.6	3.6	–2.1	–15.1
Long-term	4.3	3.9	3.3	4.3	5.8	5.7	4.6	–1.0	..
Canada									
Short-term	4.7	4.2	3.6	4.3	5.2	6.1	4.7	–1.1	–15.4
Long-term	6.5	6.6	5.9	6.4	7.7	7.1	6.7	1.2	..

1. Real short-term interest rates are measured by deducting the annual percentage change in the GDP deflator from nominal rates and real long-term rates by subtracting the low frequency component of the annual percentage change of the GDP deflator using the Hodrick-Prescott filter.
2. Partly projected.
3. Cumulated change in the effective exchange rate between the first half of 1992 and the first half of 1995.
Source: OECD.

It is difficult to evaluate the incidence of such high real interest rates and the rise in the effective exchange rate on output. Most econometric studies point to a relatively low sensitivity of consumption and business investment to real short and long-term interest rate variations. On the other hand, housing investment reacts strongly to interest rate changes. Although households are net creditors, recent estimates by the OECD suggest that the interest rate sensitivity of household spending has become more marked since the liberalisation of financial markets.[10] Very high interest rates, even if only temporary, during periods of currency turmoil can have additional effects. They raise the financing cost of inventories and short-term loans and increase the risk of bankruptcies. In addition, banks may be forced to restrict lending. *Ex post* simulations with the OECD's INTERLINK model indicate that, if the real short-term interest rate in France had been as low as in Germany between the second half of 1992 and the first half of 1995 (that is, 2 percentage points lower on average), domestic demand might have been an accumulated 1 per cent and GDP ½ per cent above their actual values by 1995. Had the exchange rate been substantially lower as a result of lower interest rates, the growth stimulus would have been considerably stronger over this period, but the acceleration in inflation due to the lower exchange rate would have had negative implications for growth over the longer term. The interest rate and exchange rate sensitivity of the French sub-model in OECD's INTERLINK model is described in Annex I.

Low inflation and a rigorous monetary policy stance can be rewarded by a reduction in interest rate differentials, thereby offsetting the effects of a strong exchange rate and high short-term interest rates. Indeed, nominal bond yields declined substantially, from close to 10 per cent in 1990 to 6 per cent in January 1994, their lowest level since 1966, and the differential against German rates narrowed from 1½ percentage points to practically zero in early 1994. However, since then bond yields have risen again sharply, mainly reflecting developments in international financial markets, but also a renewed widening of the differential against German rates. Long-term bond yields peaked in October 1994 at 8.5 per cent, before easing back to 7½ per cent in May 1995. Current real bond yields are as high as those observed during the 1980s, considerably higher than in Japan or Germany, and close to rates in the United Kingdom.

The evolution of long-term interest rates attests to the strength of international capital market integration: since early 1994, interest rates have risen OECD-wide from a low base, presumably reflecting a shift in expectations about future growth and inflation developments. The OECD's empirical work (Orr *et al.*, 1995) shows that the upward drift in rates of return on physical capital may also have played a role. Movements in real rates internationally have been closely aligned in recent years, but fairly large differentials persist across countries: while real long-term rates were below 4 per cent in Germany and Japan between the second half of 1992 and the first half of 1995, they were much higher elsewhere (Table 9). Likely explanations for such country differentials include relative fiscal and current account positions and indicators of past performance in controlling inflation. A long memory of France's earlier inflationary history probably explains part of the risk premium, and the persistence of high government deficits is adding further to it. However, as inflation is now under control, significant gains in terms of credibility could be achieved over the coming years, and with a swift cut in deficits, long-term interest rate differentials could decline and the likelihood of currency turmoil diminish. The current monetary policy setting is largely guided by the desire to move quickly towards a single European currency, and the interest rate differential against Germany points to significant potential gains for France from such a move. It is highly probable that a credible European monetary policy would yield gains over the long-run in terms of lower real interest rates.

Money and credit developments

Money growth targets play a role in providing a reference point for monetary developments in the medium-term. Until 1993, yearly objectives for the growth of the monetary aggregate M3 were announced (Figure 5). Since 1994, M3 has been set to expand at a rate of 5 per cent in the medium-term (no ranges attached), based on growth in nominal potential output of the same magnitude. Total indebtedness is being monitored closely as another important indicator. The monetary objectives are geared towards achieving price stability, which is defined as a rate of inflation below 2 per cent. These monetary objectives were reaffirmed in early 1995.

Money demand actually fell between mid-1993 and mid-1994 to the level of early 1992. The fall in M3 reflects weak activity, the persistence of high interest rates and portfolio shifts into non-monetary financial instruments. Special factors, such as the "State loan" in mid-1993 (which raised FF 110 billion) and privatisation, are also likely to have played a role, inducing a shift from M3 to

Figure 5. **MONEY AND CREDIT**

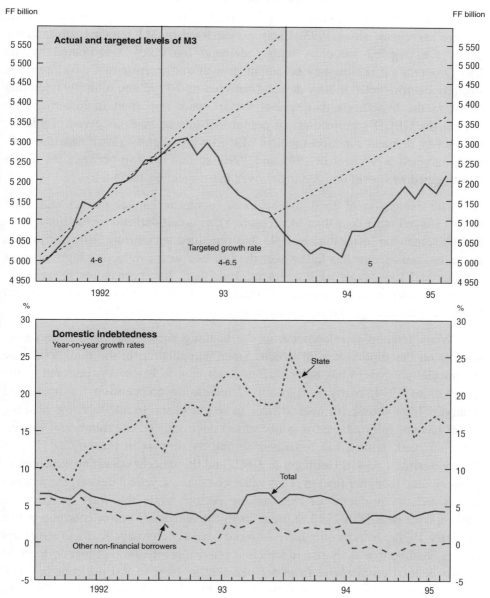

Source: Banque de France.

non-monetary assets. Monetary easing and stronger economic activity are reflected in a pick-up in the demand for broad money since mid-1994 and in the narrow aggregates since 1993. Even so, the level of M3 remains substantially below the targeted value. A money demand function[11] – estimated by the OECD – relating real money to output growth and interest rate developments, strongly overpredicted money demand between mid-1993 and mid-1994, lending credit to the hypothesis that special factors were important in lowering M3. Taking the OECD's projections of output and interest rates as given (Table 7), the money demand function predicts M3 growing slightly faster than the officially targeted 5 per cent in 1995 and 1996, so that the gap between the actual and targeted M3 level could narrow over the projection period.

The expansion of total indebtedness (domestic capital market and bank credit) slowed much less than M3 (Figure 5), as credit demand by the State, even though somewhat lower than in 1993, has remained very strong. However, credit to the business sector has fallen over the last two years, reflecting high business savings and low levels of investment. But, there has been some recovery in lending activity in recent months. Furthermore, lending to households remained weak, despite stronger housing investment and demand for durables.

Weak lending developments in the banking sector may also reflect constraints on the supply of bank credit. Since deregulation in the mid-1980s, the intermediation margin has halved, from 3 per cent to below 1½ per cent in the first half of 1994, partly as a result of increasing competition for funds and relatively high short-term interest rates in recent years. In addition, the banking sector has not fully adapted to a liberalised environment: the number of inhabitants per bank branch has remained among the lowest in the OECD (179 in France against 1 564 in Germany in 1992) and the ratio of operating expenses to gross income is higher than in many other countries. Cyclical developments have aggravated the problems of the banking sector: while the wave of business bankruptcies peaked in 1993, difficulties in the real estate sector continue. Since the early 1990s, bank profits have suffered severely from cyclical and structural factors, leading to a sharp rise in loan loss provisions: the ratio of lost or doubtful credits in total credits rose from 5.1 per cent in 1991 to 7.9 per cent in 1993. Loan loss provisions fell somewhat in the first half of 1994, but preliminary estimates suggest that the aggregate losses of commercial banks rose in 1994, with a widening dispersion of results among banks.

To a large extent the problems in the real estate sector are due to an office building boom in the *Ile de France* region in the late 1980s. With falling demand during the recession and the coming on-stream of additional capacity, rents per square metre have halved and property values dropped significantly. Rather than trying to sell on a falling market, many owners have decided to retain their investments. Vacant office space in the region is currently estimated to be between 4 and 5 million square metres. It could take years to sell or let such a quantity, and the current levels of provision only cover about half of all doubtful credits (Table 10). In order to maintain prudential ratios above the legal minimum, several banks and insurance companies have created special corporate vehicles (*structure de cantonnement*). While such structures solve balance sheet problems in the short term, they involve considerable running costs and expenses in terms of the accompanying guarantees.

Table 10. **Provisions for doubtful real estate assets**

End-1994, FF billion

	Total assets	Doubtful assets	Provisions	Provisions/ doubtful assets
Crédit Lyonnais [1]	60.1	7.9	3.8	48.1
BNP	23.9	10.7	6.6	61.7
Paribas (Groupe)	23.8	13.5	6.9	51.1
Suez (Groupe)	27.3	19.8	11.4	57.6
Société générale	23.3	7.9	4.4	55.7
Crédit agricole	18.0	8.7	5.8	66.7
Crédit foncier	13.9	7.6	4.7	61.8
Comptoir des entrepreneurs [1]	6.5	2.6	1.5	57.6
UIC [1]	10.1	5.2	2.8	53.8

1. After creation of special corporate structures. Assets hived off amounted to FF 79.5 billion for the three banks.
Source: Immo Presse.

The State has so far provided financial support to five banks and one insurance company,[12] the most important being the rescue package for the *Crédit Lyonnais*. This case is specific, as its problems also stem from a very rapid external and industrial expansion phase during the late 1980s. Some of these investments were unprofitable or credits became doubtful and losses soared from

FF 1.8 billion in 1992 to FF 12.1 billion in 1994. After a first rescue package in 1994,[13] a second package in 1995 aims at a return to profit, at avoiding distortions to competition, and at minimising the cost to the budget. It is based on hiving off into a special structure net assets worth FF 135 billion, which include the non-performing property loans of the earlier rescue, the bank's most troubled assets and its entire portfolio of profitable industrial shares. The special structure finances the asset purchase through a credit from a newly created public agency, which is itself financed by a *Crédit Lyonnais* credit. This public agency guarantees (through participating loans) the potential losses of the special structure, which will be managed by the bank under the supervision of an advisory board,[14] its aim being a rapid disposal of the portfolio. Potential losses are estimated to amount to about FF 50 billion – although considerable uncertainty attaches to this estimate – and they are expected to be covered in a number of ways: the transfer of 34 per cent (or 60 per cent above a certain limit) of the bank's pre-tax profits to the public agency for 20 years, receipts from zero coupon bonds expiring in 2014 financed by *Crédit Lyonnais*, all or part of dividend payments, receipts from the future privatisation of *Crédit Lyonnais*, and a capital injection of FF 4 billion by the State. In addition, the bank will have to shrink its balance sheet, notably by selling bank assets in other countries. If the future development of the real estate sector is favourable and if the restructuring of the bank gets underway quickly, the future cost to the public of this rescue package could be as low as officially expected. The State will not receive future dividends or the receipts from an eventual privatisation, as they will go to the newly created public agency.

The *Crédit Lyonnais* case has raised competition issues, and the European Commission is currently examining – as it does for all operations where the State is the owner – the whole package and especially whether it could distort competition in the banking sector. It has also raised issues about internal control, banking supervision and corporate governance: the current set-up appears to be unsatisfactory, as it took a considerable period of time to evaluate the size of the *Crédit Lyonnais* losses and the rescue plan was only put into place in 1994. More generally, corporate governance problems for state-owned enterprises arise where the State and public agencies choose the management, fix the business strategy, and control the outcome, while other public bodies are responsible for prudential supervision or verifying the competition implications of rescue packages.

Fiscal policy

The 1994 Budget and amendments

The 1994 Budget aimed at stringent expenditure restraint (Table 11). Outlays were budgeted to increase by no more than inflation[15] and real primary spending to fall. Revenues were estimated to rise by a little more than 2 per cent, less than projected GDP growth, and the deficit to decline to close to FF 300 billion (4.1 per cent of GDP). The Budget included a reform of personal income taxation, which reduced income tax revenue by about FF 20 billion, while the proceeds of privatisation were estimated to provide FF 55 billion.[16]

Table 11. **State budgets and outturns**

FF Billion

	1993			1994			1995	
	Budget	Budget amendments	Outcome	Budget	Budget amendments	Outcome	Budget	Budget amendments[1]
Direct taxes	585.5	548.4	546.8	535.3	549.4	545.6	566.1	576.7
Indirect taxes	974.3	906.2	882.9	922.3	917.0	919.9	960.1	974.3
Repayments	−238.7	−243.5	−220.5	−221.0	−213.7	−211.1	−220.4	−224.1
Fiscal receipts, net	1 321.1	1 211.2	1 209.1	1236.6	1 252.8	1 254.4	1 305.9	1 326.9
Other receipts	153.0	173.7	189.0	181.4	191.8	204.8	179.5	183.5
Transfers to local authorities and EC	−237.5	−238.3	−232.6	−244.1	−238.7	−236.8	−245.2	−240.2
Receipts	1 236.7	1 146.6	1 165.5	1 173.9	1 205.8	1 222.4	1 240.2	1 270.2
Compensation	510.1	510.9	509.1	525.5	531.6	531.8	542.4	549.9
Public debt	169.9	189.9	190.0	209.0	207.9	208.3	216.1	232.9
Other current expenditure	530.3	558.9	596.6	556.7	583.1	601.3	575.6	635.0
Capital expenditure	191.8	204.4	185.5	184.0	184.4	180.2	181.1	174.5
Expenditure	1 402.1	1 464.2	1 481.2	1 475.3	1 507.0	1 521.6	1 515.3	1 592.2
Déficit	−165.4	−317.6	−315.6	−301.4	−301.2	−299.1	−275.1	−322.0[2]
Memorandum items:								
Deficit (per cent of GDP)	2.2	4.4	4.4	4.1	4.1	4.1	3.6	4.1
Nominal GDP growth	5.5	2.5	1.0	3.4	3.8	4.1	5.3	5.3

1. The data refer to the draft law.
2. The Budget does not include privatisation receipts.
Source: Ministère des Finances.

Growth in 1994 turned out to be significantly stronger than expected: fiscal receipts were higher by 1½ per cent, in line with GDP growth. Receipts from privatisation were larger than projected (FF 63.7 billion against a budgeted FF 55 billion) and the difference was used to inject capital into state-owned enterprises.[17] However, additional tax revenues were not used to reduce the deficit but to increase spending. This included: the quadrupling of the school-start allowance (FF 5.9 billion), additional social spending (FF 5.6 billion), labour market measures (FF 8.2 billion) and an increased peace-keeping role (FF 4.3 billion). Overall, expenditure rose by 3.1 per cent above budgeted outlays. The deficit of FF 300 billion was close to the Budget forecast. The acceleration of VAT refunding (FF 82 billion) in 1993 and the take-over of the accumulated debt of the social security system (FF 110 billion) in early 1994 added to State debt, which rose from 30 per cent of GDP in 1992 to close to 40 per cent in 1994.

General government net lending on a National Accounts basis was considerably higher than the State's budget deficit on a Public Accounts basis (Table 12). In contrast to the Public Accounts, privatisation receipts are listed in the National Accounts not as current revenue, but as a financial transaction, and as a result the

Table 12. **Financial balances by level of government**

	1991	1992	1993	1994	1995[1]	1996[1]
	Per cent of GDP					
Net lending						
General government	−2.2	−4.0	−6.1	−6.0	−5	−4½
Central government	−1.7	−3.0	−4.5	−4.8		
Local authorities	−0.2	−0.4	−0.2	−0.2		
Social security	−0.3	−0.7	−1.4	−1.0		
	Percentage changes					
Memorandum items:						
General government						
Current receipts	4.3	3.1	2.4	4.4	5	5¾
Total expenditure[2]	5.5	6.9	6.4	4.1	3½	4
Nominal GDP	4.1	3.5	1.0	4.1	5	5¼
Real GDP	0.8	1.4	−1.5	2.8	3	3

1.   Projections.
2.   Current and net capital outlays.
Source: INSEE and OECD.

State's net borrowing actually rose between 1993 and 1994. In addition, a debt relief package for the CFA zone pushed up the central government deficit. While improving, the social security deficit did not fall by as much as expected, despite the reform of the unemployment insurance scheme and the increase in contribution rates, the creation in 1993 of the Solidarity Fund (which is financed by tax receipts), which took over certain spending functions from the social security system, and health care and pension reforms. Receipts of the general scheme were lower than expected, due to wage moderation and social security contribution exemptions for people in labour market programmes, which are not all compensated by the State. While the rise in contribution rates and cuts in generosity led to a considerable improvement in the balance of the unemployment insurance scheme, the pension and, particularly, the health insurance schemes remained in deficit. Spending on health was much lower than in earlier years, reflecting not only the effects of reform effort in the area of health care consumption, but also a rise in direct payments by patients and the absence of epidemics. When local authorities are included, both total government spending and revenues rose by close to 4½ per cent in 1994, and the government deficit/GDP ratio fell only slightly to 6 per cent (5.7 per cent excluding the debt relief package for the CFA zone countries), despite economic recovery. While the deficit/GDP ratio did not satisfy the Maastricht criterion in 1994, the gross debt/GDP ratio – at 48.5 per cent – remained below the Maastricht ceiling.

The 1995 Budget and amendments

In line with its medium-term fiscal programme, the 1995 Budget introduced by the previous Government aimed at expenditure restraint and a further fall in the deficit. Expenditures were budgeted to rise by about 2 per cent – the same as projected inflation – and the deficit to fall from 4 per cent of GDP in 1994 to 3½ per cent in 1995. Excise taxes on tobacco and gasoline were raised and privatisation was assumed to provide about FF 55 billion. Employment by the State was projected to remain stable and wages to rise by 3½ per cent, in line with the 1993 wage agreement. Expenditure restraint was budgeted to fall heavily on capital expenditure, which may have remained below its 1994 level, and on transfers to local authorities and the European Union. The cyclical improvement should also have helped in reining in the fast rise in spending on the labour market.

The amendments to the State budget include several spending initiatives in favour of employment, the housing sector and small and medium-sized enterprises. A rise in taxation will cover these initiatives as well as overspending and revenue shortfalls in the first half of the year. Spending and taxation by the State will rise FF 32 billion above the initial 1995 Budget and the deficit (adjusted for accounting changes) will remain unchanged. In order to bring budgeting procedures closer to the Maastricht definition, privatisation receipts will no longer be used to finance current expenditure[18]. On a full-year basis taxation will rise by about 1 per cent of GDP. In addition, the minimum wage and pensions were raised in July and a higher school-start allowance will be reintroduced. The new Government is committed to reducing general government net borrowing from 5 per cent in 1995 to 3 per cent of GDP in 1997.

The following spending initiatives, which would raise outlays by ⅔ percentage point of GDP on a full year basis, were announced in June:

- The implementation of the *contrat initiative-emploi* (CIE), targeted at the long-term unemployed, and the suppression of the *contrat de retour à l'emploi* (CRE) to take place in July. The *complément d'accès à l'emploi* (CAE) and a more generous *aide au premier emploi des jeunes* (APEJ) targeted at young people.
- For all employees earning between the SMIC and 1.2 times the SMIC, employer contributions will be lowered on a degressive scale (FF 800 at the SMIC, FF 400 at 1.1 times the SMIC and 0 at 1.2 times the SMIC). At the minimum wage level, the reduction in labour costs will be 10 per cent.
- The Government will provide money to renovate the social housing stock quickly in order to provide 10 000 *logements d'urgence* and 10 000 *logements d'insertion* by the end of the year. Additional tax deductions will be provided for owners renting apartments and the transactions tax (*droit de mutation*) will be reduced by 30 per cent.
- In addition to the indirect labour cost reductions, measures in favour of small and medium sized enterprises will be implemented.

As well as these spending initiatives, overspending and revenue shortfalls in the first half of 1995 (FF 49 billion) also need to be covered. Overspending was highest on interest payments, employment programmes and income support (giving an overall total of FF 23 billion), while the revenue shortfall was FF 11 billion. The initial Budget aimed at a deficit of FF 275 billion (including FF 47 billion in privatisation receipts). The new way of accounting, and overspending and revenue shortfalls resulted in a new Budget baseline of FF 371 billion.

In order to bring the deficit back on track (FF 322 billion, excluding net privatisation receipts) and finance the new spending initiatives, lower priority spending will be cut and taxes raised. The tax increases are temporary and taxes will be reduced as soon as it is clear that the Maastricht deficit criterion can be reached. The standard VAT rate will rise, from 18.6 per cent to 20.6 per cent, and corporate and wealth taxes will also be increased. Additional revenues from suppressing the income tax deduction for pension contribution payments and a rise in the *cotisation sociale de solidarité*[19] will flow to the social security system. On a full-year basis, taxation of households will rise by nearly FF 70 billion and enterprises will pay an additional FF 20 billion.

On the basis of the amended 1995 budgetary statements and with some improvement in the social security deficit from the 1994 level and a small deficit for the local authorities, general government net borrowing could be 5 per cent of GDP in 1995. For 1996, the OECD's projection is based on the assumption of strong expenditure restraint and no change in taxation. This could lead to a further fall in the overall deficit, to 4½ per cent of GDP in 1996. Additional measures, especially in terms of continuing health care reform, are likely to be needed in order to achieve the assumed expenditure restraint.

The OECD's fiscal indicators suggest that the rapid deterioration in the fiscal situation between the late 1980s and 1993 was largely due to cyclical factors, with the sharp rise in interest payments and policy changes playing a more modest role (Figure 6). The expected improvement in the deficit between 1993 and 1996 again owes more to cyclical developments than policy tightening, while the snowball effect of fast rising debt levels on interest payments is hindering fiscal consolidation. If the new Government does not tighten policy significantly, efforts to reduce the deficit – as measured by the change in the cyclically adjusted primary deficit – will look pale on an international comparison: without further policy action the French deficit/GDP ratio may fall by 1½ percentage points only between 1993 and 1996, the structural component contributing ¾ percentage point, in the United Kingdom the cut in the deficit could amount to 5¼ percentage points over the same period, the structural component contributing 4 points, and in Germany the decline could be 1 percent-

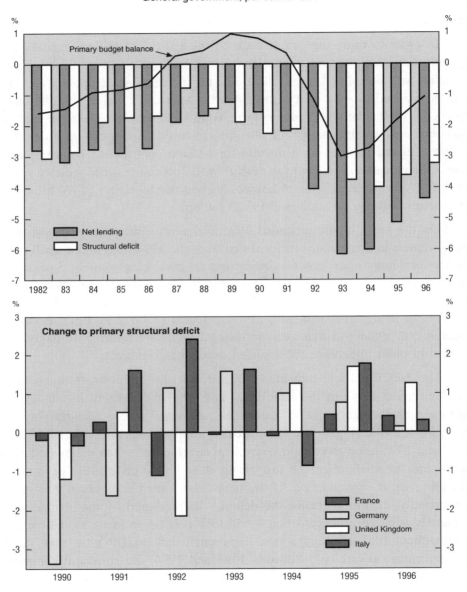

Figure 6. **INDICATORS OF FISCAL STANCE**

General government, per cent of GDP

age point, the structural component contributing 2 percentage points.[20] On this basis, Germany and the United Kingdom would fulfil the fiscal Maastricht criteria in 1996, but this is not the case for France, Italy, or the European Union on average. However, the Maastricht debt criterion will be easily met in France, and in this respect France is in a better position than Germany and the United Kingdom.

Medium-term and long-term fiscal considerations

An important plank in the Government's strategy is the move to European Monetary Union. In order to achieve the necessary deficit reductions, multi-annual deficit and spending targets for the State were introduced in 1994, aiming at a State deficit of 2½ per cent of GDP by 1997 (including privatisation receipts) and at an increase in the State's spending of no more than inflation. The deficit target, as set out in the medium-term fiscal plan, was respected in 1994. However, expenditure grew considerably faster than inflation, and higher than expected receipts were not used to accelerate the reduction in the deficit, as stipulated in the medium-term programme. In addition, the State's deficit rose on a National Accounts (Maastricht criterion) basis.

Apart from the deficit and spending objectives for the State, the previous Government aimed to meet the Maastricht target by cutting the general government deficit to 3 per cent of GDP by 1996. According to the convergence programme, the general government deficit should have been reduced to 5.1 per cent of GDP in 1994 and 4.2 per cent in 1995. The new Government has set a revised deficit reduction path: 5 per cent of GDP in 1995, 4 per cent in 1996 and 3 per cent in 1997. According to the OECD's medium-term scenario, which assumes no further policy initiatives and projects growth of real GDP of around 3 per cent, an additional effort will be needed to achieve the official objective of a deficit of 3 per cent of GDP in 1997. This effort needs to be shared by all levels of government, including local authorities: over the last cycle, their expenditure rose twice as fast as State outlays. In the OECD's medium-term scenario, the debt/GDP ratio, on a Maastricht basis, will remain below 60 per cent and start to fall from 1998 onwards.

The OECD's projections, which include a fair amount of expenditure restraint – a rise of 1.8 per cent in real public expenditure over the projection period as compared with an increase of 3.3 per cent between 1980 and 1994 on average – show a difference of FF 110 billion between the deficit (4½ per cent of GDP) and the Maastricht target for 1996. The Maastricht criterion in 1997 can only be achieved through large expenditure cuts. These can only be found by pruning big ticket items: the government wage bill and social spending. There appears to be room for reining in expenditure on both. The share of total government employment in total employment is among the highest in the OECD area: in 1990 it was close to 23 per cent as compared to 15 per cent in Germany and the United States.[21] Streamlining of operations should be possible and objectives in terms of government employment could be fixed. Moreover, wage increases in the public sector have outstripped private sector wage gains by a considerable margin over the last few years. While base rates have moved roughly in line with private sector rates, promotions and career measures, often phased in over many years, have raised average salary growth significantly. In addition, social security rate increases have a smaller incidence on the take-home pay of public officials, as they do not pay unemployment insurance contributions and contribute less than private sector employees to their pension scheme. Since 1991, their take-home pay has risen by close to 3 per cent in real terms, compared with less than 1 per cent for private sector employees. Moderate public sector salary increases will be a necessary component of expenditure restraint beyond 1995.

The previous Government provided several scenarios for financing the social security general scheme[22] for 1995 to 1997: they are all based on revenue growth of 3½ per cent in 1995 and 5½ per cent in 1996 and 1997. Expenditure growth in the reformed pension scheme is expected to be somewhat above 4 per cent between 1995 and 1997. Assuming that health expenditure grows in line with GDP, which implies a continuation in the change in spending trends since 1993, the total deficit would fall to FF 37.5 billion in 1997. Spending growth would need to slow to 2 per cent in nominal terms by 1997 in order to balance the general scheme by 1997. The latter scenario would imply extremely stringent expenditure restraint on health care, which appears difficult to attain without a binding budget constraint. In addition, the revenue assumption in these scenarios could be optimistic, as lower social security contributions by certain segments of the labour market are only partially compensated by the State. However, since 1994, the State has had to compensate any revenue shortfalls due to new employment programmes.

There is a clear need to pursue reforms of the social security system vigorously. In this respect, significant progress has been made in curbing health expenditure for ambulatory care. Apart from a further increase in the patient's contribution, agreements[23] on annual spending caps with private clinics, biologists, nurses and physiotherapists have been in force since 1992, and with pharmaceutical companies and doctors since 1994. Medical guidelines (212 are in force), which define norms and include penalties, have been established. It was decided to introduce individual medical files between now and 1997. While it is difficult to differentiate between the impact of these measures and the slowdown in the growth of real income, it is clear that expenditure growth on ambulatory care has decelerated appreciably since 1992 (Table 13). It is still too soon to assess the long-term effects of the 1994 agreements, but experience with earlier reforms shows that a slowdown can be followed by a return of expenditure growth on ambulatory care to its earlier trend rate, if expenditure control is not pursued strenuously. In addition, in order to assess doctors' performance and encourage preventive medicine, it was decided in May 1995 to introduce computerised coding of treatment and diseases before the end of 1996. Initially the coding will concern biologists and pharmacists, and should serve as a basis for reimbursement.

In contrast to ambulatory care, little progress was made in the hospital sector and spending growth has accelerated since 1992, despite the June 1993 increase in direct payments by patients (Table 13). Excess capacity in hospitals has been reduced only a little. An information system concerning hospital costs and spending (*programme de médicalisation des systèmes d'information, PMSI*), which had been introduced on an experimental basis as early as 1982-83, was generalised in public hospitals in late 1993. This system should lead to budgets being allocated on the basis of medical activity as of 1996.

Long-term scenarios concerning the impact of demographic changes on future pension, health and education spending also highlight the need for further reforms of the health and pension systems (OECD, 1995*d*). French population growth is likely to slow until 2030 and remain stable thereafter, while the ratio of the retired to the working age population could rise from 37 per cent in the year 2000 to 63 per cent in 2030. The reform of the general pension scheme in July 1993 was a first major step in the right direction.

Table 13. **Expenditure ceilings in the health sector**

Percentage changes in nominal terms

	1980-85	1985-90	1992		1993		1994		1995
			Target	Out-come	Target	Out-come	Target	Out-come	Target
Public hospitals	12.6	6.0	5.0	7.0	5.2	6.2			
Private hospitals	13.6	7.0	5.2	6.8	4.4	6.3	3.4	−3.4	3.1
Biologists	16.2	9.9	7.0	4.7	4.9	0.8	0.8	−8.2	
Nurses	19.3	13.0	9.7	7.7	7.4	4.5	3.6	3.7	
Physiotherapists	16.6	9.7	..	5.6	..	2.7		2.9	
Doctors	14.6	9.2	..	5.8	..	4.4	3.4	1.9	3.0
Pharmaceuticals	13.8	8.4	..	6.2	..	7.1	3.2		
Dentists	11.9	8.1	..	5.4	..	3.3			
Memorandum items:									
Total health									
expenditure	13.7	7.7		6.6		5.7	5.7	3.4	
Excluding									
hospitals	14.5	9.3		5.7		3.8	3.4	1.9	3.0
Consumer prices	9.4	3.0		2.4		2.2		1.8	

Source: SESI, *Comptes nationaux de la Santé*, 1991 à 1993; Soubie *et al.* (1994).

This reform[24] focused on gradually reducing the generosity of pension payments. The measures, including the shifting of the payment of non-contributory old-age insurance benefits to the old-age solidarity fund (*Fonds de solidarité vieillesse* – FSV),[25] should prevent further rises in social security contribution rates until 2010. In contrast, the supplementary pension schemes have decided to increase their contribution rates every year between now and 1999-2001 so as to maintain the level of pension payments. According to the national old-age pension fund (CNAV, 1995), the gross overall replacement rate (including supplementary schemes) will fall by 7 points to 65 per cent for men by 2015, but will increase by 2 points to 70 per cent for women.[26] The real financial return on social security pension operations, *i.e.* the average rate of interest at which an employee's contributions would have to be invested in order to earn a monthly income equal to his/her social security pension, is expected to fall by 2 points on average, to 2 to 2½ per cent in 2015. Furthermore, while systems akin to pension funds already exist for some professional groups, the introduction of funded systems for all employees is still being discussed by government and the social partners.

40

In contrast to the pension system for private sector employees, plans to reform the special old-age pension schemes have not been announced. Yet the cost of these schemes, which apply to both civil servants and employees of most state-owned companies, is increasing as a result of unfavourable demographic trends.[27] The solidarity link between systems, which was established in 1974, means that the social security system and the State budget help in financing the special schemes. However, the differences between these systems, in terms of benefits and conditions of access to pensions, are considerable and are more favourable to the special schemes, with the result that there could be problems of fairness – particularly since private sector employees will see the rate of return on their pensions decline between now and 2014.

While the reform should keep the general pension scheme close to balance until 2010, the ageing of the population and a fall in the working age population could lead to a rapid erosion of the financial soundness of the pension system thereafter: without further measures it could move from close to balance in 2010 to a deficit of 4 per cent of GDP in 2030[28] (Table 14). Several policy options to contain the rise in the future pensions system deficit have been simulated by the OECD:

- Lifting the retirement age: the pension age in France is currently at the low end compared with the other large OECD countries, many of which have phased in a rise in the pension age.[29] Increasing the pension age by five years would bring it into line with practice in other countries, and would generate considerable savings by increasing the working age population and reducing the elderly dependency ratio. This would bring the scheme close to balance. A rise in the years of contribution as in the 1993 reform appears to be only a partial substitute for an increase in the statutory age: a recent study by the pension system administration (CNAV) shows that lengthening the period of contribution has not increased the effective pension age. Policies discouraging participation, such as early retirement schemes, should be overhauled.
- Raising contribution rates: a rise of 10 percentage points on top of the current rates, which are already very high, would be needed to close the financial gap.[30]
- Reducing generosity: the simulation results suggest that generosity needs to fall by more than 10 per cent in order to resolve the financing problems.

Table 14. **The impact of demographic changes on future government spending**

	2000	2015	2030
Baseline simulation			
Elderly dependency ratio	36.9	47.6	62.7
Total dependency ratio	84.3	92.1	110.8
Pension expenditure/GDP ratio	9.4	10.4	13.1
Primary balance/GDP ratio	1.5	0.3	−3.8
Net lending/GDP ratio [1]	−1.6	−2.1	−8.5
Net debt/GDP ratio [1]	41	37	88
Pension policy options (balance of the pension			
system as a per cent of GDP)			
Baseline [2]	−0.2	−1.1	−3.8
Replacement rate 10 per cent lower	−0.2	−0.2	−1.2
Contribution rate 3 percentage points higher	−0.2	0.0	−2.7
Retirement age 5 years later	−0.2	2.4	0.1
International comparaison			
Net lending/GDP ratio [1]			
United States	−2.2	−3.3	−9.3
Japan	−2.0	−10.5	−19.8
Germany	−1.9	−2.1	−9.4
Italy	−3.5	−3.5	−12.8
United Kingdom	0.1	0.9	1.0
Canada	−0.1	3.1	−1.1

1. Interest rate/growth rate differential held constant.
2. Fictive public sector contributions amounting to 1.7 per cent of GDP are included.
Source: OECD, *Economic Outlook,* No. 57.

In the absence of reform, higher spending would lead to larger primary deficits and a rapidly rising debt. According to the OECD's simulation, which takes the rather optimistic fiscal situation of its medium-term scenario as a starting point, the overall deficit could rise from 1½ per cent of GDP in 2000 to close to 8½ per cent by 2030. Net debt levels would surge from 40 per cent of GDP in the year 2000 to close to 90 per cent in 2030 (Table 14). The simulated deterioration in French public finances is about the same as in Germany, but much smaller than in Italy or Japan. A better starting point – a higher primary surplus in the year 2000 – would generate a significantly more favourable debt dynamic and would help confront the fiscal problems posed by ageing in the absence of pension reform.

The results of the simulation exercises should be regarded as indicative only – they are an attempt to illustrate the effects of demographic developments on future government spending and not projections of future developments. How-

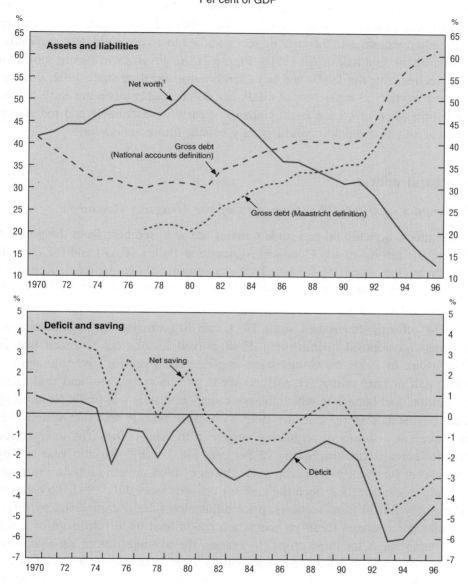

Figure 7. **GOVERNMENT NET WORTH AND SAVING**

Per cent of GDP

1. INSEE's net worth calculation is based on unconsolidated assets and liabilities.
Sources: OECD and INSEE.

ever, they clearly show the importance of pursuing fiscal consolidation with much more ambition than in the second half of the 1980s. Then deficits were reduced only to levels that just stabilised the debt/GDP ratio, and the subsequent sharp deficit increases in the ensuing recession led to a very rapid debt accumulation during the first half of the 1990s (Figure 7). As government saving showed a trend decline over the 1980s and has even became negative since 1992, government net worth,[31] as a per cent of GDP, has fallen steeply since the early 1980s. The continuation of such a fiscal course is clearly unsustainable and redressing the fiscal situation quickly would greatly benefit future generations.

Structural policies

The impact of the CAP reform and of the Uruguay Round

France's agricultural and trade policies are analysed here from the point of view of the reform of the Common Agricultural Policy (CAP) and the conclusion, under the April 1994 Marrakech Agreement, of the Uruguay Round of multilateral trade negotiations, which led to the setting up of the World Trade Organisation (WTO).

The reforms undertaken since 1984, and in particular the introduction of maximum guaranteed quantities in 1988 proved insufficient to reach market equilibrium. In 1991, the Commission implemented a reform covering approximately half of farm output (cereals, oil seeds, protein crops, beef and veal, lamb and mutton, and butter), in which the price support system was partly replaced by direct payments starting with the 1993-94 harvest year. A set-aside system was introduced as a means of regulating supply in the short term. The intervention price for cereals was lowered by 25 per cent for the 1993-94 crop year and by 6.7 per cent for the 1994-95 crop year. Prices of high protein crops are now set by world markets, as has been the case for oilseeds since July 1992. To counterbalance any fall in farm incomes, price adjustments are accompanied by direct subsidies per hectare. These payments are conditional upon fulfilment of a set-aside requirement for three crops. In France, the average rate of set-aside was 13.8 per cent in 1993 and 15.5 per cent in 1994.[32] Intervention prices in the livestock sector were reduced by 5 per cent in July 1994, the fall being compensated by an increase in direct payments (subsidies for cows feeding their calves and for male cattle).

Support in the area of agricultural policy occurs at two levels. First, Community funding of agriculture was based mainly on market price support until 1992, with institutional prices being set at levels well above world prices, variable import levies and export subsidies. For many products, these policies were accompanied by measures aimed at limiting the volume of output benefiting from the price support system. With the reform of the CAP, which aimed at compensating lower prices with direct assistance, community financing almost doubled between 1990 and 1993, rising from 28 to 41 per cent of aid to agriculture[33] (Table 15). The most important and rapidly increasing subsidies concern "productive" agricultural activities which received 84.5 per cent of European funding in 1993. The main items of Community assistance responsible for this rise are subsidies for cereals[34] and the increase in direct forms of support as of 1992 (see above). The second strand of farm sector aid measures relates to spending by the French authorities, which, unlike the CAP, is mainly on structural measures[35] and social protection for farmers, in particular pension payments. In early 1995, it was decided to lower social security contributions so as to make it easier for farmers to adjust to the new trading environment resulting from the Uruguay Round agreements. Another recent agricultural law, passed in early 1995,

Table 15. **Breakdown of agricultural subsidies**[1]

FF billion

	1990	1991	1992	1993	1994[2]
Agricultural produce	51.7	58.1	62.6	83.9	72.1
Agro-food industry	1.1	1.0	1.0	1.1	1.3
Other[3]	3.8	4.0	4.9	5.5	5.1
Research, education and general services	12.1	12.9	14.0	14.7	15.1
Social protection	64.1	66.3	69.9	73.8	73.8
Total	132.8	142.5	152.3	179.0	187.3
of which:					
EAGGF[4]	37.2	47.0	53.0	73.5	60.6
National financing	95.6	95.5	99.3	105.5	126.7

1.   Excluding cross-subsidies for cereals and milk.
2.   Provisional.
3.   Horses, forest products.
4.   European Agricultural Guarantee and Guidance Fund.
Source: Ministère de l'Agriculture et de la Pêche.

included tax expenditure and measures aimed at helping young farmers to start up. Between 1990 and 1993, domestic support for agriculture, which is funded mainly from the BAPSA (supplementary budget for farm sector social benefits), increased by 10 per cent. Because of demographic trends and the relatively low level of farmers' contributions,[36] transfers from the central government and the social security scheme account for 80 per cent of BAPSA resources.

Farm output in volume fell by 2 per cent in 1993 – largely due to the set-aside programme – and remained virtually flat in 1994. While the fall in agricultural produce prices[37] has started to benefit user industries, so far the impact on retail food prices has been less apparent. Although their rate of increase slowed from 3.4 per cent in 1992 to 1 per cent on average in 1993-94, there is still room for a reduction in food prices in France, as their level is much higher than in the EU on average, or in Australia and the United States (Table 16). According to official estimates, the reform of the CAP should allow a slow rise over the medium term but was unlikely to have much effect on farm incomes in 1993; they fell by $1/2$ per cent in 1993, and then rose by 11.5 per cent in 1994 (mainly due to income generated in markets not targeted by the reform). The surplus on agri-food trade shrank by FF 11 billion in 1994, to FF 45 billion. This decline is due to the sharp rise in imported raw material prices, a lower surplus earmarked for export and lower wheat export prices. On the other hand, the fall in the surplus was cushioned by a rise in the amount of domestic cereals used for animal feed, made possible by lower domestic prices.

Table 16. **Comparison of food prices**

1990[1]

	France	Germany	United Kingdom	EC-12	United States	Japan	Australia
Food products	100	96	79	93	73	143	72
Bread and cereals	100	97	72	92	86	151	94
Meat	100	93	68	89	59	159	50
Fruit and vegetables	100	97	86	85	76	123	65
Beverages	100	93	129	99	102	195	136

1. Comparative price levels at international prices, including indirect taxes. A potential list of 630 goods are included, of which France priced 460.
Source: OECD, *Purchasing Power Parities and Real Expenditures.*

Agriculture was one of the main issues during the Uruguay Round of trade negotiations. The compromise reached in 1994 should ensure compatibility with the CAP reform. The EU countries are required to reduce their subsidised exports by 21 per cent in volume and their direct export subsidies by 36 per cent, from 1986-90 levels. It is planned to spread these reductions over time, so that exports do not decline too rapidly after the agreement comes into force. The measures in the agricultural agreement will be phased in over six years and, thus far, it is difficult to gauge their impact, particularly since trends in world markets and in exchange rates will largely determine the extent of the reduction. In the OECD's view (OECD, 1995) the CAP reform is likely to reduce the EU-wide wheat and cereal surpluses available for export. Cuts in support prices and the scheduled reduction in the surface of farmed land ought to curb cereal production and increase domestic consumption, thereby reducing the surpluses available for export. It is also difficult to assess the medium-term impact of the CAP reform on the Community's beef and veal market. Uncertainty exists about the future compatibility of surpluses available for export and the measures agreed in the Uruguay Round concerning subsidised export volumes. The effects of the Uruguay Round agreement on the trade balance are difficult to evaluate: while restrictions on export volumes should start to be binding from 1995 onwards for certain products, unsubsidised exports on certain market segments could rise helped by stronger world market prices. In this respect, the rising surplus of manufactured food products should be noted. The 1995 trade balance will strongly depend on the development in import prices, especially of tropical products.

The other Uruguay Round measures which particularly concern France aim at lowering the level of protection in sectors where they have remained high in the EU or trading partner countries. These measures largely concern declining domestic industries and export sectors having to contend with tariff differences in other countries. The present agreement provides for:

- the complete abolition of customs duties in eight industrial sectors,[38] and the harmonisation of duties on chemicals. These measures should boost exports in these nine sectors, which, in 1992, accounted for 16½ per cent of total exports outside the EU and had a trade surplus of FF 29 billion;
- an average one-third reduction in other duties. Community protection is virtually unchanged for the automobile industry and remains the same for consumer electronics and aluminium. On the other hand, duties on semi-conductors were cut appreciably. The most significant liberalisa-

tion will be in the textiles sector, with the gradual dismantling of the Multifibre Arrangement (MFA) over a period of ten years and its incorporation in the GATT rules.

A multilateral agreement on government procurement, which should increase competitive pressures, has been signed by the EU and twelve other countries, including the United States. Progress on intellectual property rights[39] should have beneficial effects for France, particularly as there are measures for confiscating counterfeit goods at the boarder. The cost of counterfeiting, apart from the direct misappropriation of sales (loss of earnings), is put at almost 3 per cent of the total sales of the industries concerned, particularly the luxury goods industry. According to a study by the firm of McKinsey, the French luxury goods industry accounted for 47 per cent of the world market in 1989. A 1985 report by the European Parliament put the number of jobs lost in France at 20 000 (100 000 in the European Community and 130 000 in the United States). The number at present is put at 30 000 by the Ministry of Finance.

One of the major breakthroughs of the trade negotiations is the extension of the GATT rules to services. Trade in services accounts for a growing share of international trade, and France is the second biggest net world exporter of non-factor services after the United States. In the General Agreement on Trade and Services (GATS), countries undertook to apply the Most Favoured Nation (MFN) clause to all their partners. Rules were laid down concerning the opening up of certain sectors (financial services, telecommunications, airline services), while a list of commitments defines ways in which each country may limit market access and avoid compliance with the MFN clause. Some topics are still being discussed – the aeronautics industry, financial services, maritime transport and telecommunications – and there is a cultural exception clause for television and protectionist measures in the audio-visual industry. The agreement on services preserves the whole body of Community regulations and allows the national treatment principle to be taken as a reference. The preferential market access arrangements accorded to third countries, notably for professional services, remain in place.

Land use planning

Land use and territorial development policy aims to compensate inequalities in living conditions arising from geographical location and its demographic and economic consequences. In this respect, it should be noted that the per capita income spread in France was the second highest in the EU in 1989, behind Italy (Cingolani, 1993).

The December 1994 Guideline Act on territorial development is designed in particular to reduce differences in incomes across regions, bringing them all to between 80 and 120 per cent of the per capita national average by 1997. Redistribution of financial resources between regions and between municipalities, which began in 1991, is to be stepped up as of 1995. In addition, tax allowances are being awarded to firms on the basis of their location.[40] Similarly, exemption from taxes on profits for new firms is now reserved for those locating in certain priority areas. A corporate development fund (FF 2.3 billion, of which 0.65 billion comes from a government grant, while the remainder comes from EU loans and from borrowing) has been set up to provide loan guarantees and to grant loans to SMEs. A new land development scheme is to be drawn up in late 1995, while four sectoral development plans are to be introduced in mid-1996 in the following areas: cultural amenities, communications, health care organisation and higher education and research. To speed up infrastructure development, two funds[41] have been set up to ensure redistribution in the air and land transport sectors (FF 0.16 and 2.1 billion, respectively, see below).

Competition policy

There has been only a very gradual implementation of the measures contained in the Community directives to improve competition. In the case of telecommunications, only value-added services such as mobile telephones and radio-paging have been deregulated (1986). Voice telephony should be liberalised and its infrastructures opened up to competition by late 1997. Neither the details nor the timetable of a possible privatisation of *France Télécom* have as yet been defined. As far as rail transport is concerned, infrastructure and services are gradually being separated, but solely on an accounting basis. The State retains responsibility for the infrastructure, while the SNCF remains as manager and user. However, as the SNCF was authorised in May 1995 to make its cable network available to private operators, *France Télécom* no longer has a monopoly on the infrastructure. There has been no deregulation in the energy sector, France's position – which is to keep its monopoly on electricity distribution – being very different from that of the Commission. In the insurance sector, the regulations have been amended to incorporate in French law the provisions of the third life and non-life insurance directives of mid-1994; insurance companies can distribute their products throughout the EU and prudential rules have been strengthened.

The legislation on the opening of new supermarkets has been slightly relaxed, with stricter administrative requirements replacing the freeze on permits. The regulations on the siting of retail outlets in urban areas have not prevented a large increase in the number of supermarkets and the overall surface area of hypermarkets has more than tripled since 1973. Under the tighter legislation brought in 1990 (*Loi Doubin*), the construction of new outlets slowed in 1991 and 1992, but this was more than offset by the extension of existing superstores. However, the freeze on permits for new retail outlets did significantly curb the increase in shop floor area in 1993,[42] but this could also be due to the effects of the recession. In addition, in the multi-annual employment programme of December 1993, Sunday opening laws were relaxed for recreational and leisure activities.

Industrial Policy

Since 1993, the main focus of industrial policy has been on privatisation, with a series of asset sales involving firms in the competitive sector and financial institutions, totalling FF 114 billion (Table 17). The privatisation procedure provides for the constitution of a hard core of firms which undertake to hold blocks of shares for a minimum period of time. In order to build up share ownership and involve employees in the success of its privatisation, employees enjoy certain specific advantages, most notably a minimum quota representing 10 per cent of the securities placed on the market, discounts and payment facilities. The Government also has the right to restrict some buyers' participation in asset sales. Except in the case of sales of Renault shares, the State is either no longer a shareholder or has kept only a very limited part of the capital of privatised firms. The privatisation of Bull has been delayed by difficulties in finding a group of major investors. *Usinor-Sacilor* was privatised in June and other asset sale operations should be announced during 1995.

The other important component of industrial policy concerns assistance to the business sector, notably small enterprises. In 1994 the Government took a number of measures aimed at encouraging the creation and expansion of small

Table 17. **Privatisations in 1993-95**

	Receipts FF billions	Share of sold assets	Share of remaining assets
1993 Total	**47**		
of which:			
Crédit local de France	2	18	8
Total	2	3	5
Rhône-Poulenc	16	43	0
BNP	27	73	0
1994 Total	**61.8**		
of which:			
ELF-Aquitaine	33.7	44	11
UAP	18.8	50	0
Renault	8.4	29.9	50.1
1995 Total			
(as of 30 April 1995)	**5.5**		
Seita	5.5	90	10

Source: Ministère des Finances.

businesses. The main items in this package include equality of legal treatment between small businesses and companies, the simplification of administrative procedures and improved access to local saving *via*, for example, tax reductions for people investing in small businesses. Measures have been taken, in particular, to lighten the cost of and improve social protection for the self-employed (craftsmen, shopkeepers and entrepreneurs), reduce the burden of taxation, protect the assets of unincorporated enterprises and simplify administrative procedures.

III. Labour market policy in the 1990s

With the recent improvement in employment, the unemployment rate has fallen from its peak of 12½ per cent in mid-1994 to 11½ per cent in the spring of 1995 (2.9 million unemployed). This is the same as the average rate in the European Union, but higher than in the OECD area as a whole (8 per cent) (Figure 8). According to OECD estimates, three-quarters of unemployment is due to structural factors. In addition, there were 1.5 million beneficiaries of job support schemes in 1993.

Unemployment has risen in stages over successive cycles, accompanied by an increase in the number of long-term (over one year) unemployed. Since 1990, the share of the latter in the total number of jobless rose by 4½ points to 35¾ per cent in 1994, which is not, however, among the highest in the EU.[43] Furthermore, the labour market is characterised by the particularly acute problems that the young, women and the least-skilled workers experience in finding employment. Youth and, to a lesser extent, female employment rates are particularly low in France (Figure 9). While the youth unemployment rate fell over the period 1985-91 in line with the increased number of job schemes targeted at this age group, in 1994 it was almost as high again as in the mid-1980s owing to the decline in the number of beneficiaries of labour market programmes and the slowdown of activity (Table 18). In 1994, more than half of all young people were not in work, while only a quarter were in jobs paid at market rates. Youth unemployment was almost twice the adult rate because of the decline in the labour force as a result of the raising of the school leaving age, but the proportion of unemployed in the 16-25 age group was only 10.2 per cent. While the female unemployment rate is markedly higher than that for males, the ratio of the two rates fell from 2.8 at the start of the 1970s to 1.4 in 1993. The unskilled unemployment rate rose by 7½ points between the two cyclical peaks in 1981 and 1991, to 21½ per cent in 1993, compared with the overall unemployment rate of 11.7 per cent (Table 19).

Figure 8. **LABOUR MARKET DEVELOPMENTS**[1]

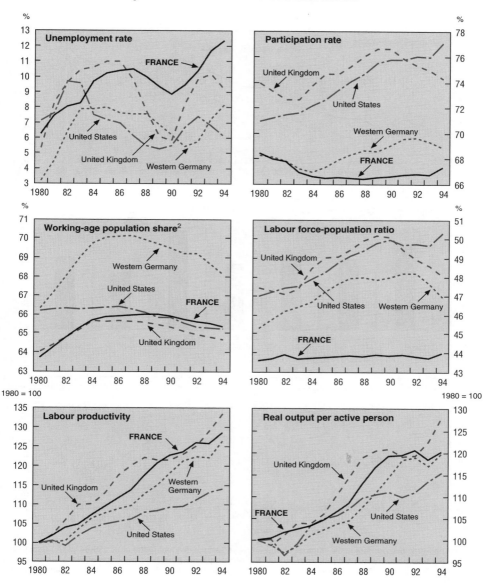

1. The unemployment rate is related by an identity to the other five factors displayed.
2. As a percentage of total population.
Source: OECD, *Labour Force Statistics* and estimates.

Figure 9. **LABOUR UTILISATION IN FRANCE**

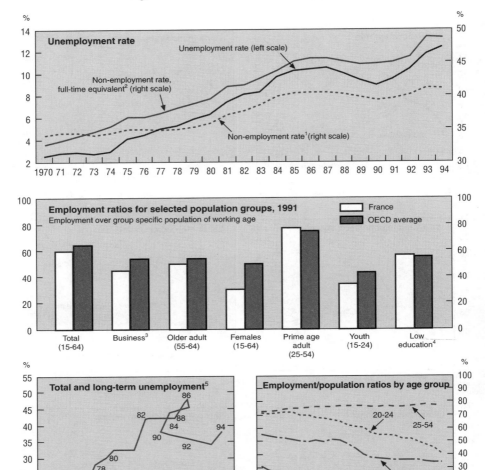

1. The non-employment rate is the number of non-employed adults divided by the adult (15-64 years) population.
2. The full time non-employment ratio recalculates the non-employment ratio on the basis of actual annual hours worked relative to a 40-hour week and a 48-week year until 1981 and a 39-hour week and 47-week year after 1982.
3. Business sector employment divided by working age population.
4. Individuals aged 20-64 years who have not completed upper secondary school.
5. People looking for work for one year or more as a per cent of total unemployment.
Source: OECD.

Table 18. Main characteristics of youth activity

Shares of population aged 16-25, in March

Per cent

	1983	1985	1987	1989	1991[1]	1993	1994
In employment	46.8	42.8	42.7	40.7	40.6	37.7	33.9
Assisted by specific measures	5.3	5.6	10.8	8.9	8.5	9.4	7.3
Apprenticeships	2.6	2.5	2.6	2.7	2.6	2.3	2.7
Other (including trainees)	2.7	3.1	8.2	6.2	5.9	7.1	4.6
Unassisted	41.5	37.2	31.9	31.8	32.1	28.3	26.6
National service	2.9	2.9	2.7	2.7	3.2	3.0	2.8
Unemployed	9.8	12.4	11.2	8.7	7.7	9.4	10.2
Non-active	36.7	38.6	40.3	43.3	48.2	49.3	50.8
In education	29.9	32.0	34.6	38.2	42.8	44.4	45.7
Others	6.8	6.6	5.7	5.1	5.4	4.9	5.1
Residual	3.8	3.3	3.1	4.6	0.3	0.5	1.4
Memorandum item:							
Unemployment rate	18.9	23.7	21.7	17.9	17.4	22.2	23.2

1. Care should be taken in comparing 1991 with earlier years as the methodology changed.
Source: INSEE, *Première* and *Enquêtes sur l'emploi.*

Table 19. Unemployment according to occupational category and the cycle[1]

Per cent

	1974	1975	1982	1985	1991	1993
	P	T	P	T	P	
Farmers	0.1	0.2	0.2	0.5	0.6	0.6
Craftsmen, traders and entrepreneurs	0.6	1.3	2.0	3.0	2.5	4.5
Senior management and professionals	1.0	1.7	2.5	2.9	3.0	4.9
Intermediate-category professions	1.1	2.1	4.1	4.5	4.2	5.8
Non-manual workers	2.8	4.5	8.9	10.8	11.6	13.9
Manual workers	2.1	4.1	9.6	13.7	11.6	14.4
of which:						
Unskilled	..	..	11.3	15.8	18.8	21.5
Skilled	..	..	6.7	10.8	7.2	10.2
Total (including the unemployed who have never worked)	2.8	4.9	8.1	10.2	9.4	11.7

1. Standardised unemployment rate. P: peak of the cycle; and T: trough of the cycle.
Source: INSEE, *Marché du Travail, séries longues,* 1994, and *Enquête sur l'emploi de 1991.*

The rise in unemployment, its causes and the response of the authorities, were the subject of a special chapter in the 1991/1992 OECD Economic Survey of France (OECD, 1992). The present chapter consists primarily of an analysis of the policies implemented in this area since the beginning of the 1990s in the light of the OECD's recent work (OECD, 1995*b*).

The main objectives of labour-market policies

In response to mounting unemployment, the authorities have stepped up labour-market initiatives since 1989, with increased emphasis on active labour-market policies rather than on cushioning the social effects of unemployment (Table 20). Public expenditure on labour-market support rose from 2.6 to 3.4 per cent of GDP (by value) from 1989 to 1993, with a sharp acceleration since 1991, while private funding[44] remained at ³/₄ per cent of GDP over the same period. In 1992 public expenditure was much higher than in the other major OECD countries with the exception of Germany, which had to cope with the structural adjustment problems resulting from unification (Table 21). Expenditure on labour-market policies increased by 28 per cent in real terms between 1989 and 1993. Unemployment benefits rose by 19 per cent and expenditure on active measures to promote employment by 51 per cent. On the other hand, as early retirement schemes were scaled back, expenditure on measures to encourage withdrawal from the labour force fell by 40 per cent between 1989 and 1993 (and by 53 per cent from 1987, the year it was the highest).

The focus of labour market policy was gradually shifted to measures to promote employment. The share of expenditure on such measures in 1993 was nonetheless still smaller (48 per cent) than that on passive measures to help the unemployed and to promote early retirement. For public expenditure alone, the share of active measures was 33 per cent in 1992 (28 per cent in 1989), slightly below the OECD average (Table 21). The number of beneficiaries of active job support schemes increased from 750 000 in 1989 to 1¹/₄ million in 1993. Expenditure on job creation schemes virtually tripled in real terms between 1989 and 1993. In terms of numbers employed, the main scheme of this type is the "employment-solidarity contract" (*contrat emploi-solidarité* – CES) in the public sector. The number of beneficiaries of this scheme has risen steeply in the 1990s, to reach a stock of 437 000 in March 1995. The CES are essentially for

Table 20. **Employment support expenditure: some indicators**

	1973	1980	1987	1989	1990	1991	1992	1993	1994
A. Total expenditure [1]									
FF billions	10.2	64.8	192.3	202.1	218.2	239.0	261.7	288.8	
In constant 1990 prices	38.8	119.2	211.5	208.9	218.2	231.6	247.7	267.6	
As a per cent of GDP	0.9	2.3	3.6	3.3	3.3	3.5	3.7	4.1	
Per employee									
FF thousands	0.5	3.0	10.2	10.4	11.0	12.0	13.3	14.8	
In constant 1990 prices	1.9	5.4	11.2	10.7	11.0	11.7	12.6	13.6	
B. Total expenditure by nature, share in per cent	100.0	100.0	100.0	100.0	100.0	100.0	100.0	100.0	100.0
Passive	34.1	57.6	62.8	59.5	57.1	56.3	55.0	52.2	
Unemployment benefit	18.6	40.4	37.1	39.2	40.1	42.6	44.0	42.6	
Early retirement	15.5	17.3	25.7	20.3	17.0	13.7	11.0	9.6	
Active	65.9	42.4	37.2	40.5	42.9	43.8	45.0	47.9	
Employment maintenance	1.4	3.9	1.5	1.3	1.6	1.5	1.6	2.2	
Job creation	4.9	4.1	7.6	5.6	6.7	7.7	8.7	11.9	
Incentives to labour-force participation	0.8	2.1	2.0	2.0	2.1	1.9	1.7	1.8	
Professional training	56.2	30.6	24.8	30.0	30.9	31.0	31.2	30.3	
Other	2.6	1.6	1.4	1.5	1.7	1.8	1.8	1.7	
C. Beneficiaries of labour-market programmes [2]	91	619	1 731	1 484	1 538	1 592	1 707	1 919	
Early retirement	44	188	470	344	288	235	199	180	188
Unemployed exempt from job search	0	0	141	220	230	233	233	252	285
Professional training for the unemployed	47	87	151	206	237	247	275	333	
Private-sector subsidised employment	0	344	767	547	634	665	724	782	970
Public-sector employment contracts	0	0	202	167	149	212	276	372	407

1. Public and private expenditure, including professional training financed by enterprises.
2. Average annual stock in thousands.
Source: Ministère du Travail.

57

Table 21. **International comparison of public
labour-market expenditure**

1992

	Per cent of GDP	Share of "active" measures
France	2.99	32.8
United-States [1]	0.69	34.8
Japan [2]	0.35	25.7
Germany	4.19	37.7
Italy	1.84	50.5
United Kingdom [1]	1.75	29.7
OECD [3]	1.72	33.7

1. 1993-94.
2. 1992-93
3. Simple average.
Source: OECD, *Employment Outlook,* July 1994.

young people, the long-term unemployed and women. Other schemes provide for exemptions from social security contributions, which are paid by the government,[45] for apprentices, unskilled young people and the long-term unemployed.

On the one hand, employment policy has sought to lower the cost of the least-skilled and those facing the greatest difficulties in finding employment, to develop training and apprenticeships, and to promote labour market flexibility. On the other hand, steps have been taken by the social partners to make the unemployment insurance system less generous, with the dual aim of reducing the deficit and increasing incentives to look for work. These aims have been restated and amplified in a five-year programme on labour, employment and training, which was adopted in December 1993 and is centred around job creation, work organisation, training and entry into employment.

Lowering the cost of labour

The share of wages in value added has fallen sharply since 1982, and unit labour costs do not appear higher than the European average. However, the convergence of wage costs has been achieved at the cost of high unemployment, the employment-wage rate breakdown of the wage bill being particularly unfavourable in France. While the increase in the real wage bill was very similar in Germany, the United States and France between 1978 and 1994, in France the breakdown between employment and wage increases has been essentially to the detriment of employment (Figure 10).

While the overall level of unit labour costs in France is not high, relative to other countries, labour costs for the unskilled do seem to pose a particular problem. The level of unemployment among the least skilled workers points to a mismatch between the cost of labour and marginal productivity and, in this connection, there have been a number of studies on the impact on employment of the cost of the minimum wage. Although some of them do not show that such systems have a negative impact, they concern countries where the minimum wage is well below the average wage. In France, on the other hand, the level of the minimum wage (SMIC)[46] in relation to the average wage is the highest in the OECD after the Netherlands, although in the latter country there are significant age-related reductions in the minimum wage. Also, the ratio of the SMIC to the average wage has remained practically unchanged since 1988, whereas it has been falling in most other countries. In summary, the SMIC does appear to have an appreciable impact on unemployment among the least skilled workers, and especially the young (Figure 11). The problem is clearly one of the cost of labour at the SMIC level, 49 per cent of which is social security contributions. The reduction in contributions to the family allowance and health insurance schemes will lower this rate to 35 per cent. A study on youth employment commissioned by the Senate has concluded that a 20 per cent reduction in the SMIC could, in the medium term, result in the hiring of 136 000 young people, but this improvement would be to the detriment of employment among the not-so-young, so that the net effect on total employment would be only 30 000. The French authorities have not sought to lower the level of the minimum wage, which is seen as contributing to social cohesion. There was an unsuccessful attempt in spring 1994 to make the minimum wage more flexible. The problem of the cost of the SMIC has, however, been side-stepped by means of the fairly systematic reductions in social security contributions, introduced in various labour-market programmes, which have led to lower labour costs without reducing the take-home pay of a *Smicard* (*i.e.* a person in receipt of the SMIC).

Measures have been taken to reduce the cost of the least-skilled workers, notably the young and the long-term unemployed. In the private sector "re-employment contracts" (*contrats de retour à l'emploi*, or CRE) have grown in

Figure 10. **REAL COMPENSATION AND EMPLOYMENT**

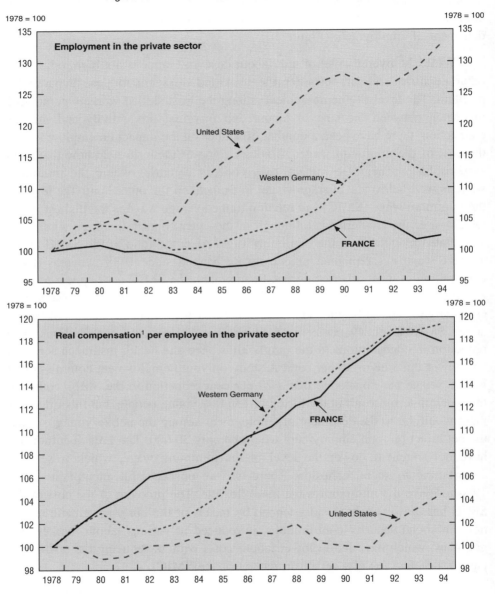

1. Deflated by the private consumption deflator.
Source: OECD.

Figure 11. **UNEMPLOYMENT RATE AND MINIMUM WAGE**

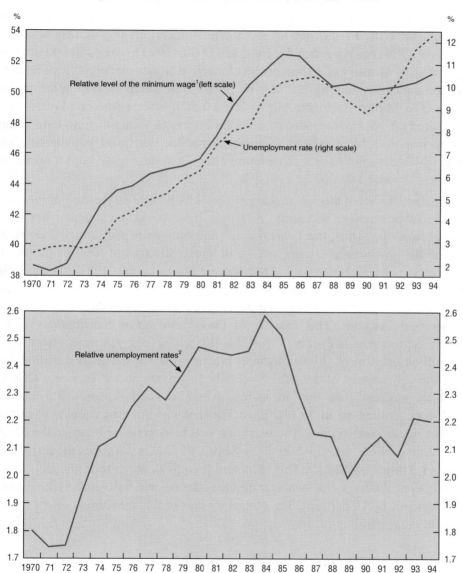

1. The ratio of the minimum wage (SMIC) to the average wage.
2. The ratio of youth to total unemployment rate.
Sources: INSEE and OECD.

61

importance. They are reserved for the long-term unemployed and give employers total exemption from social security contributions – with the State bearing 90 per cent of the cost. In the public sector the number of employment-solidarity contracts (CES) has risen rapidly, from 150 000 in 1990 to over 400 000 in 1994. According to Ministry of Labour estimates, active labour-market policy measures reduced unemployment by 221 000 in 1991-93, of which 84 000 in the private sector. The Ministry estimate allows for windfall effects (the employer would have hired labour anyway) and substitution effects (a young or long-term unemployed person is hired instead of someone outside the target population). The CES, which does not have a substitution effect, had the bigger impact on unemployment – some 140 000 in 1991-93.

In order to avoid the substitution effects which occur in the case of targeting specific labour-market segments, measures have been taken which are more general in scope. Thus, the financing of contributions to the family allowances scheme for low income earners will be progressively moved from employers to the central government budget. This process began in mid-1993 and by 1998, wages less than 1.5 times the SMIC will be totally exempted from these contributions,[47] and wages between 1.5 and 1.6 times the SMIC will receive a 50 per cent discount. This transfer of family allowance contributions to the central government budget will cost FF 30 billion per year and affect some 7½ million employees. Lower indirect labour costs for the least qualified will raise the job content of growth, especially in private sector services. Official estimates suggest that this measures, which concerned some 3.5 million employees, created about 70 000 jobs. The new Government decided to reduce indirect labour costs further. The reduction will be degressive between the SMIC and 1.2 times the SMIC (FF 800 at the SMIC, FF 400 at 1.1 times the SMIC and zero at 1.2 times the SMIC). This reduction is equivalent to the employers' social security contribution to the health insurance scheme, and will reduce labour costs for a *Smicard* by 10 per cent. The budgetary cost of this measure is FF 19 billion on a full-year basis.

Enterprise-based training and apprenticeship

The average level of education has improved, but the difficulties that young school-leavers have in finding employment point to the need to improve training, whether it is provided by the education system or at the workplace. Numerous schemes, which target unskilled young people and combine school and work-place training together with reductions in the cost of labour, have been introduced. The reductions in labour costs are granted to businesses that take on a person who would have difficulty finding a job at the market wage rate, the employer receives a reduction in social security contributions and, in some schemes, a subsidy. While various enterprise-based training schemes for young people still co-exist, the five-year programme on employment has streamlined and reduced their number.

Enterprise-based training schemes, apart from apprenticeship, do not seem to generate more net job creations than those schemes which provide only exemption from employer contributions, insofar as the reduction in the cost of labour plays a preponderant role in both types of schemes. Once the windfall and substitution effects have been allowed for, net job creation could represent about one-fifth of gross hirings (Table 22). Of the various types of work-based schemes, the "skill formation contract" (*contrat de qualification*) has been the most effective in terms of net job creation (30 per cent of gross hirings). However, it should be noted that a large proportion of the young people participating in this scheme are already educated to the level of the *baccalauréat* or higher. The training credit scheme tailored to individual needs (*crédit formation individualisé* – CFI), in which 530 000 young people enrolled over the period 1990-93, is aimed at young people who have left school without a qualification and who have failed to find a job. It is a package which can comprise several periods of practical training and also courses. According to a Ministry of Labour survey, 29 per cent of participants in a CFI in 1992 had obtained a qualification by the end of the course, while 42 per cent had found a job six months after completing the scheme.

In contrast to Germany, apprenticeship still plays an inadequate role in training in France. It is primarily used to train craftsmen and workers in the private service sector. In addition, only relatively low qualifications are necessary to attain a diploma and some 50 per cent of apprentices receive one. Apprenticeship generates substantially more net job creations than other types of enterprise-based training schemes (accounting for 70 per cent of gross hirings since 1985). However, it has little appeal for young people, and in response to the stagnation in the number of apprentices, the starting age was lowered to 14 years in the multi-annual employment programme. Furthermore, the 1993 Budget introduced,

Table 22. **Ex ante assessment of some youth employment programmes**

Employment creation in thousands, full-time equivalent stocks

	1985	1986	1987	1988	1989	1990	1991	1992
Private sector[1]								
Gross	13.8	213.4	479.2	215.5	158.0	169.2	168.0	213.9
Net	4.4	33.4	82.0	59.8	41.1	42.6	43.2	48.1
Substitution effect	4.5	68.6	157.5	71.2	49.6	48.7	44.5	57.5
Windfall effect	4.9	111.5	239.6	84.5	67.3	78.0	80.1	108.2
Public sector[2]								
Gross	65.1	101.1	98.9	92.8	78.0	58.5	65.3	84.9
Net	65.1	101.1	98.9	92.8	78.0	58.5	65.3	84.9
Apprenticeship								
Gross	55.8	57.5	65.6	74.2	77.8	77.7	77.7	75.2
Net	37.1	40.2	45.9	51.9	54.4	54.4	52.6	52.6
Total								
Net	108.6	174.7	226.8	204.5	173.4	155.4	161.1	185.9
As a per cent of gross								
employment creation	81	47	35	53	55	51	52	50
of which: private sector	32	16	17	28	26	25	26	23

1. *Plan d'urgence pour les jeunes* (1986-88), *Exo-jeunes* (since 1991), *Exonération pour le premier salarié* (since 1989), *Contrat de qualification* (since 1985), *Contrat d'adaptation* (since 1985), and *Stage d'initiation à la vie professionnelle* (1985-92).
2. TUC and *Jeunes volontaires* (1985-90) and *Contrat-emploi solidarité* (since 1990).
Source: Cette *et al.*, 1993.

with retroactive effect from 1992, a system of tax credits for firms that take on additional apprentices. These measures are likely to have contributed to the rise in apprenticeships in 1994 (250 000 against 200 000 in 1993). The efforts to promote apprenticeship could run into funding problems, as only part of the apprenticeship tax (0.5 per cent of the wage bill) is earmarked for this type of training, the rest being used to finance other schemes, including those at post-secondary level.

Increasing labour flexibility

In addition to active labour market policies, a number of measures have been introduced to facilitate labour market adjustments. Greater flexibility may involve increased recourse to part-time work. Since September 1992, partial exemption from employer social insurance contributions has been granted for hiring a part-time worker on an indefinite-term contract, and for switching an employee to part-time work in order to avoid a redundancy.[48] The growth of part-time work was amplified by the raising of the rate of exemption from 30 to 50 per cent in 1993. The rate was lowered again to 30 per cent in the five-year employment programme in April 1994, but this does not seem to have slowed the growth of part-time contracts. Since 1994, the range of hours that can be worked on a part-time basis has been widened.[49] Most part-time workers are women (accounting for nearly nine out of ten part-time jobs) and youth employed by small firms in the service sector. According to a survey conducted by the Ministry of Labour in March 1994, this measure seems to have given rise to substantial windfall effects, three-quarters of firms saying that they would have recruited in any event. With or without exemption, part-time employment has expanded rapidly. Its share of total dependent employment rose from 12.3 to 14.3 per cent between 1991 and 1993, and to 15.4 per cent (3.2 million) in 1994.

In addition to incentives for part-time work, the redistribution of working hours is an important part of employment policies. The five-year employment programme aims to make working hours more flexible. For example, the regulations concerning the maximum number of hours worked in a week have been eased. On the other hand, the programme gives employers and unions the opportunity to conclude decentralised agreements with a view to calculating working hours on an annual basis, and encourages them to do so by providing subsidies for that purpose. Such agreements reduce the cost of overtime, improve the utilisation of capital and often enable job cuts to be avoided. Yet, it would seem that very few of them have been signed to date.

Also, a new long-term partial unemployment mechanism (TRILD – *temps réduit indemnisé de longue durée*), which increases the number of compensated hours worked for employees on short-time working, offers an alternative to redundancies.[50] It involves the unemployment insurance scheme in the active management of the labour market since it is partly financed by it. On official estimates, this mechanism made it possible to save 10 000 jobs in 1994. As a result of the reform, compensation for short-time work is now more a matter of insurance or collective coverage, as in Italy, than of labour flexibility, as in Germany (Béraud, 1994).

On the other hand, job protection legislation has only changed marginally recently. On various composite indicators of the stringency of job protection standards in OECD countries, France ranked among the average in 1989 (OECD, 1995*b*). The cost and difficulties involved in laying off established workers were not particularly punitive, but fixed-term contracts were among the least flexible in the OECD area, while interim work was more flexible than the average (Grubb and Wells, 1993). Nevertheless, this type of legislation increases labour costs and can very well reduce the overall level of employment, indeed, the employment rate is generally not as high in countries where there is strong job protection (OECD, 1995b). It can also encourage employers to use types of contracts that allow them to lay staff off more cheaply.

Reform of unemployment benefits

Unemployment compensation can also contribute to the worsening of structural unemployment. High net replacement rates probably give wage-earners less incentive to look for work. Also, the duration of benefits can influence the length of unemployment.[51] Studies of the exit rates from unemployment show that they are high during the first months of unemployment and rise again as the expiry date for benefits approaches.

In response to the increase in unemployment and the growing difficulties of financing the unemployment insurance system, measures were taken in 1992 and 1993 to shorten the maximum duration of benefits (which is still among the highest in the European Union) and to introduce a phased reduction in benefits so as to encourage the jobless to look actively for employment.[52] Also, the benefit payment period varies according to age and the length of prior affiliation to the unemployment insurance system, the latter having been raised appreciably under the reform, so that there is less temptation to switch from being employed to being unemployed. Under the basic scheme, benefit is paid, with a lag, at an initial rate of 57.4 per cent of the gross reference wage (but almost 70 per cent in net terms) for 9 months, and is then reduced by 17 per cent every 4 months for 21 months, so that it is down to 27.2 per cent after two years. Since benefits cannot fall below a minimum rate (which is at present almost FF 4 000 before deductions), the net rate of benefit, if the reference wage is the minimum wage, is in fact equal to more than 80 per cent of the SMIC. When they are no longer entitled to unemployment benefits, the long-term unemployed qualify for a solidarity allowance which is payable on a renewable six-monthly basis.

This reform has radically changed the system of unemployment benefit payments. According to a study by the Ministry of Labour, it made possible savings of FF 7 billion in 1994 as a result both of the diminishing rate of payment and the exclusion from the scheme of recipients who had not been affiliated for long enough. Indeed, the number of jobless drawing benefits fell by 8.3 per cent in 1994, from 70 per cent of the unemployed on an ILO basis in 1993, to 59.7 per cent in 1994, while those in the solidarity scheme increased sharply (by 13.8 per cent in 1994). It is thought that some 100 000 people were excluded from the unemployment insurance scheme in 1993 because they had not contributed for long enough. Lastly, the average rate of benefit is believed to have fallen from 54.3 per cent in 1991 to 51.7 per cent in 1994, while gross average monthly benefits per head have decreased by 10 per cent in real terms from the level of the early 1990s.

Also, a guaranteed minimum income (RMI) was introduced in 1989 for persons without any means. The number of beneficiaries of the RMI rose extremely quickly to 907 000 at the end of 1994, of whom 60 per cent were registered as unemployed. The fast rise is partly due to the introduction of the degressive payment of unemployment benefits. Although the RMI amounts on average to less than FF 2 000 per month, to this must be added family allowances and housing benefits. This package can constitute a "floor wage" insofar as it is a disincentive to take a job which would not provide a sufficiently high income. According to the French employers' association (CNPF), in June 1994 the ratio of replacement income (RMI and social benefits) to disposable income for a worker paid at the SMIC was 68 per cent for a bachelor and 90 per cent for a couple with two children.

Early retirement schemes, which have existed since 1961, gradually evolved towards a broader coverage and a higher generosity ratio up to 1987. Their focus was then gradually changed: many schemes were scrapped and income support was progressively abolished. Early retirement schemes are now financed by the unemployment insurance system or central government via the *Fonds national pour l'emploi* (FNE). The unemployment insurance system finances a measure for laid-off employees of 58 years and over, and provides benefits until the pension age or a return to employment, it closely resembles an early retirement scheme. An employee who has taken early retirement receives a benefit that may not exceed 85 per cent of the reference salary. In return, the enterprise must either take on a new employee or make a financial contribution.

Furthermore, through the FNE, "gradual" early retirement benefits are targeted at employees over 55 whose full-time jobs are transformed, with their agreement, into part-time jobs, thus increasing the incentives for part-time work (see above). Although the number of beneficiaries of gradual early retirement benefits has risen steeply since 1992, they represented only 11½ per cent of the total number of early retirees in 1994. In addition to the early retirement incentives, a great many employees are concerned by the measures accompanying the restructuring of enterprises. In 1994, for example, nearly 150 000 people took leave to train for alternative employment or signed a State retraining contract.[53]

Other measures

In order to make employment policy more effective, measures were taken recently to simplify and rationalise these schemes, the number of which is excessive. The aid for the unemployed who set up a firm, for example, is now paid as a lump sum, and the conditions of eligibility have been widened. The subsidy in the form of the re-employment contract (CRE) for the long-term unemployed was modified in 1994. Some programmes have been retargeted at those sections of the population whose situation is the most insecure. For example, the conditions of eligibility for subsidised employment in the public sector have been changed and targeted at hard core unemployment and RMI beneficiaries.

The payment of social insurance contributions by households employing domestic workers was simplified with the introduction in December 1994 of the *chèque emploi-service*. This facilitates the administrative formalities and payment of wages, and should reduce the amount of undeclared work. While it is still too early to gauge exactly the impact of this measure, it does seem that it has helped to create new needs among households.

Other measures have been introduced which make it possible to take training leave and parental leave as of the birth of the second child (July 1994), but leave and breaks in career are on a much smaller scale than in Belgium or Denmark (OECD, 1995c).

The authorities also took steps in 1994 to reduce the inefficiency caused by the lack of co-ordination between the body that administers unemployment benefits (UNEDIC), the state placement and job information system (ANPE), and the management of active labour market programmes.[54] The inspectorate-general for social affairs advocates closer co-operation between these first two bodies, rather than merging them. The difficulties involved in a merger would seem to derive in particular from the difference in status (the ANPE is public and the UNEDIC semi-public), and the fact that the benefit system is partly managed by the social partners. Information has now been pooled and, in some *départements*, it is now possible to register with the UNEDIC as looking for work, and no longer solely with the ANPE. Also, a closer check will be kept on the jobless to determine whether they really are looking for work by setting up a joint ANPE/UNEDIC file. However, the monopoly of the ANPE has not been called into question.

Impact of employment policy and future trends

It is probably too soon to try to assess the impact of all these reforms, and especially the measures designed to increase flexibility and strengthen the incentive to work. On the other hand, the development of active policies has triggered a number of studies aimed at gauging the net effects of the different employment support schemes. Most of these studies point to the existence of strong substitution effects (between categories of recipient), windfall effects (employers would have recruited in any case) and incentive effects (the very existence of the programmes encouraging recipients to join the labour force). The net job creation effects range from 20 to 40 per cent of the gross effects concerned, depending on the programme (Gautié *et al.*, 1994).

In the private sector the net number of jobs created by youth job schemes probably averaged a fifth of the gross number of hirings. In terms of net job creation, some of these schemes are more effective than others. One of the youth employment schemes (*exo-jeunes*) provided, within the limits of the SMIC, total exemption from employers' contributions for a year and made possible the hiring of 68 000 young persons in 1991-92, but it had relatively little net effect – around 15 per cent. In contrast, another scheme (*contrat de qualification*) had a net effect of 30 per cent, probably due the fact that, in addition to an exemption from employers' contributions, it provided a subsidy in return for training the young people that were hired. Public sector schemes are, for their part, little affected by substitution and windfall effects, but it is difficult to assess their impact in terms of lasting entry into the labour market. Ministry of Labour estimates suggest that the increase (some 280 000) in the number of beneficiaries of overall labour market support policies meant 85 000 fewer jobless in 1993, two-thirds of these resulting from active employment subsidy measures.

These, however, are only the "quantitative" effects, which take no account of the positive effects in terms of employability and integration. Also to be taken into consideration is the assistance that firms, and particularly SMEs, receive in the form of the reduced production costs made possible by these schemes. Another factor is the cost of these programmes in relation to their effect on employment and the skills they generate. For example, it is estimated that a beneficiary of a job scheme in the private sector cost over FF 25 000 in 1993 (Table 20). The cost to public finance of all these employment support schemes can be put at nearly FF 20 billion in 1993, of which FF 12 billion was transferred from the central government budget under the heading of compensatory payments to the social security scheme.

In addition to this programme-based microeconomic approach, there have been a number of studies gauging the macroeconomic effect – *via* improved competitiveness and the substitution of labour for capital – of the reduction in the labour costs. A comparison by the *Commissariat Général du Plan* (1994) of the results of the main models shows that the five-year effects on employment of a reduction of FF 10 billion in employers' contributions vary between 38 000 (Mosaique, OFCE) and 42 500 (METRIC, Ministry of Finance). The same type of exercise can be used to calculate the effect on employment of different forms of taxation. According to these studies, employers' contributions clearly have the most punitive impact on employment and any substitution of these contributions by other taxes would have beneficial effects. The choice between indirect taxation (VAT or the tax on oil products) or direct taxation (*contribution sociale généralisée*) seems less obvious. However, alternative financing by VAT would have a slightly less favourable impact, as the inflationary consequences would limit the gains in competitiveness.

The new Government's employment policy is based on strengthening targeted measures and on extending the shift of social security contributions on low wages from employers to the budget. Several schemes aim at creating new jobs by means of a targeted reduction in small, labour-intensive firms' social security costs, encouraging the hiring of young people and combating long-term unemployment. The CIE (*contrat initiative emploi*, or employment initiative contract) will involve exemption from employers' social insurance contributions for two years at the SMIC level, plus a subsidy of FF 2 000 per month for every long-term unemployed person hired in the private sector. It is expected that approximately 350 000 people will benefit from the CIE every year – almost twice the number of CRE (*contrat de retour à l'emploi*) beneficiaries in 1994. Once it is fully operational, the gross cost of the CIE should be FF 21 billion per year, or FF 14 billion in net terms, bearing in mind the abolition of comparable schemes such as the CRE (FF 1.6 billion in 1993). Another scheme (*complément d'aide à l'emploi des jeunes*) was also created: an enterprise hiring a young person in difficulty for at least 12 months, or one with a diploma, who has been unemployed for more than three months, for at least 18 months, receives a subsidy of FF 2 000 per month for 9 months. In addition, subsidisation of apprenticeships will continue, and the subsidy raised from FF 7 000 to FF 10 000. In a full year these measures for the young will cost FF 5 billion. The Government's stated target is to increase employment by 1 million over three years. By comparison with the OECD's medium-term projections, this would mean employment picking up by a further $\frac{1}{2}$ percentage point per year and, assuming no change in the labour force, the unemployment rate falling to 9 per cent in 1998, compared with 10 per cent in the projections.

IV. Economic aspects of transport sector policies

Public policy in France has for many years placed a considerable emphasis on the development of transportation infrastructure and the delivery of transport services. This has resulted in extensive transportation networks of generally high quality, with capacity keeping pace with demand and (with the partial exception of the North-South axis and the road network in and around Paris) limited congestion.

Against this favourable background, transportation policy is facing a number of difficult, interrelated challenges: the costs to the public budget of providing transport infrastructure, and also covering operating deficits of certain segments of the transport service industry, are large – putting a premium on achieving higher efficiency. At the same time, EU-wide liberalisation is sweeping the transport sector, entailing much greater competition within and across transport modes and creating difficult adjustment problems for certain transport companies, while necessitating new approaches to managing, financing and regulating the industry. Finally, there is the challenge of devising a coherent transportation policy strategy that integrates cost considerations, environmental and congestion-related externalities, and regional policy objectives. The key in this regard may be to find ways of bringing the prices of transport services closer to their social costs, both to assure an efficient utilisation of existing infrastructure and to provide an undistorted (or less distorted) basis for evaluating the returns to additional infrastructure investments. The more efficient the transportation sector and the lower the cost, the broader the geographic markets will be. Wider markets in turn translate into greater competitive pressures, and hence greater efficiency and higher consumer welfare.

These issues are by no means unique to France. Most OECD countries are facing similar issues. It is, however, the case that France is among the countries that have been relatively conservative in shifting transportation policy away from the traditional approach of direct public provision towards the more market-oriented systems emerging from liberalisation and deregulation, so that the issues are particularly topical. This chapter first reviews overall developments and policy issues. Transport policies and developments are then discussed in greater detail in a sectoral context.

Overall developments and policy issues

Overall developments[55]

The transport sector, while small in terms of value added, just 4 per cent of GDP in 1993,[56] is significant in other respects. For instance, household outlays on transport (to a large extent car purchases and utilisation) amounted to close to 18 per cent of total consumption. The sector also generates large flows between the public and private sectors. At close to FF 200 billion in 1993, government spending accounted for close to 5 per cent of total public outlays, while government revenues related to transport activity amounted to FF 148 billion. Government spending includes public infrastructure outlays, which amounted to about 1 per cent of GDP in 1993, one-third of which was undertaken by public enterprises. In France, transport infrastructure is generally of a very high technical quality and well developed in terms of network lengths.

Road transport is the most important means of transport (both in terms of value added and passenger and tonne kilometres), mainly because of its flexibility and convenience, and its importance has increased over time (Table 23). Air transport has also gained market shares, reflecting a high income elasticity. Since the mid-1980s, the transport sector has grown faster than the overall economy and shown both faster employment and productivity growth. Sectoral changes in favour of road and air transport were even more rapid than earlier. Sizeable relative price changes also point to a significant amount of restructuring since the mid-1980s.

Compared with other European countries, the road and rail networks are considerably longer, which may be partly explained by the lower population density and the size of the country. However, part of the current rail network is under-utilised[57] and utilisation of the road network is lower than in the other large European economies (Figure 12), congestion being confined to large agglomera-

Table 23. **Overall developments in the transport sector**

1985-94 average growth rates

	Rail	Road	Air	Total	
				Transport	Economy
Output	−1.6	3.2	5.8	2.8	2.1
Modal share [1]	11.7	41.5	13.8	..	..
Employment	−2.9	1.5	1.2	0.6	0.3
Productivity	1.4	1.7	4.6	2.2	1.9
Prices	1.9	1.8	−4.4	1.0	2.9

1. Share in value added. The remaining 33 per cent comprise fluvial and maritime transport, pipelines, storage, ancilliary services and travel agencies.
Source: OEST.

tions and the North-South axis.[58] Overall highway traffic density is much lower than in Belgium, Germany, the Netherlands or the United Kingdom.[59] Congestion appears to be a lesser problem than in many other countries.

A flurry of studies since the late 1980s has attempted to demonstrate the importance of infrastructure investment for long-term growth (Gramlich, 1994). Early studies on the United States, based on simple macroeconomic production functions, suggested that public capital formation has a very high impact on aggregate output. In this framework, lower outlays on infrastructure since the mid-1970s could largely explain the trend decline in productivity. The results implied very high marginal rates of return and pointed to a severe shortage of public capital. Further research showed that the evidence for such a shortage in the United States is at best mixed. An OECD study (Ford and Poret, 1991) including several countries came to the same conclusion and did not find that infrastructural outlays had a significant effect on total factor productivity in France. Contrary to the United States, infrastructure capital stock growth was considerable in France and the ratio of infrastructure capital to output continued to rise slowly between 1970 and 1992 (Figure 13) On the other hand, Laguarrigue (1994) does find a high and significant output elasticity for transport infrastructure capital for France.[60] In addition to the difficulty of establishing a robust link between infrastructure and growth, the direction of cause and effect is not clear. Also important in this context is the evolution of the rate of return on various projects. With the rapid extension of the motorway and high-speed train

Figure 12. **NETWORK SIZE AND UTILISATION IN INTERNATIONAL COMPARISON**
1991

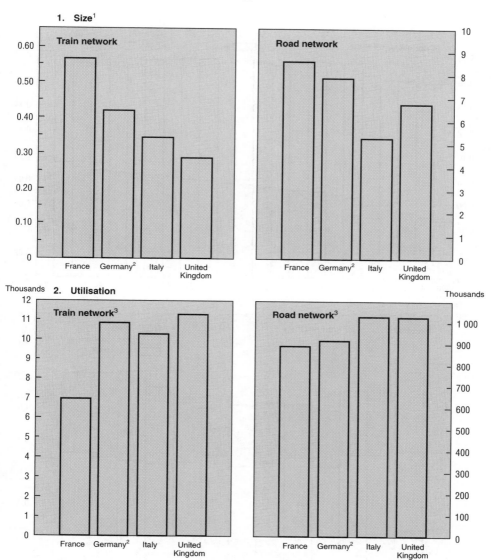

1. Size[1]

Train network

Road network

Thousands 2. Utilisation   Thousands

Train network[3]

Road network[3]

1. Network length per capita, in meters.
2. Western Germany.
3. Kilometres travelled in relation to the network length.
Sources: SNCF, UN, INFRAS/IWW (1995).

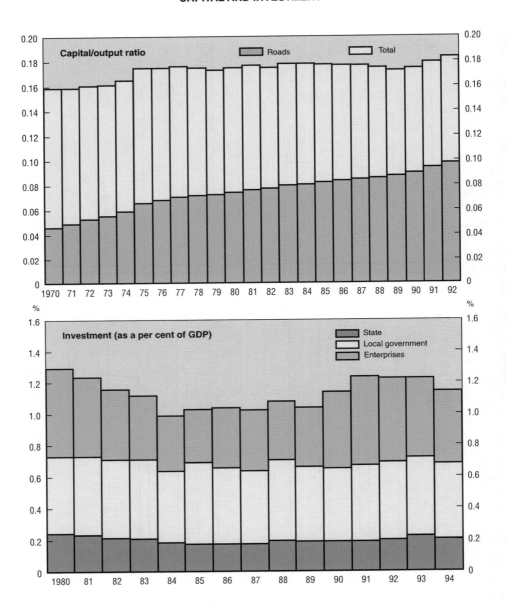

Figure 13. **TRANSPORT SECTOR INFRASTRUCTURE CAPITAL AND INVESTMENT**

Sources: Laguarrigue (1994) and OEST (1994).

networks, rates of return have tended to fall and estimated profitability for most future projects is low (see below).

The institutional setting has evolved

Until the early 1980s, the transport sector was heavily regulated and decision-making centralised. Since then, policy has changed, due to EU-wide liberalisation and the devolution of decision-making, while public service and regional policy aspects have remained important in policy-making. Since 1982, transport policy has been guided by the Act on Inland Transport (LOTI),[61] which aims at decentralisation and establishing the contractualisation (*Contrat de plan*) of relations between decision makers. The contracts between the State, the regions and the SNCF (*Société Nationale des Chemins de Fer* – the state-owned railway company), for instance, contain agreements concerning investment and its financing, the amount of compensation for running unprofitable lines (at a given price and schedule) and financial performance over a number of years. The contents of such contracts vary widely across sectors: contracts with cities other than Paris include incentives to invest in low-cost transport modes, on the other hand, no contract has ever been concluded with the RATP (*Régie Autonome des Transports Parisiens* – the Parisian public transport company) and large deficits are financed *ex post*. Such contracts have improved the general transparency and accountability of decision making and drawn a clearer line between the commercial activities of state-owned enterprises and their public service obligations. While this is an improvement on the earlier situation, it is less than perfect in some respects. Contracts do not provide sufficient incentives to minimise cost, and are difficult to design, as information is asymmetric and problems of moral hazard and regulatory capture may occur (Curien and Jacobzone, 1993). In addition, regionalisation of road planning has made decision-making less transparent and often cumbersome.

At the EU level, the Treaty of Rome (1958) aimed at the implementation of a common transport policy,[62] which was seen as an important vehicle for opening up intra-EU trade. Progress in implementation was slow and only gathered steam with the internal market initiative which pursued the liberalisation of transport services and the application of competition rules. Although the internal market is now in place, some measures remain to be phased in and derogations from competition rules still exist. In many instances, EC directives only set minimum and/or maximum rates for taxes and road tolls, and national subsidies, even though vetted by the Commission for distortionary effects, have continued to flow in ample amounts. In addition, the prices of some transport services can be set at low levels in order to achieve regional and social policy objectives (public service obligation). So far EU-wide transport policy has been largely geared towards resolving internal trade and competition (access and pricing), labour-related and safety issues. Infrastructure planning, extra-EU trade and the internalisation of externalities have received less attention so far. However, externalities received wide coverage in a recent White paper and EU-wide infrastructure planning received a boost recently, as the Treaty on European Union provides for the extension and improvement of trans-European networks. Planning of European networks complements the drawing-up of national master plans (*schémas directeurs*), the current planning horizon for motorway and railway investment being 2005. These plans are indicative and do not fix priorities or time scales for projects.

The policy issues: an overview[63]

A most important aspect of transport sector activity in almost all countries is the pervasiveness of government intervention. In addition to the railway sector, which was nationalised in 1937,[64] and transport infrastructure, which is largely provided by the Government and public enterprises, exit, entry, pricing and operating rules for many transport modes are still subject to some form of government regulation in France, even though intervention in services provision has been scaled back since the mid-1980s. Market failures would argue for a strong state presence for efficiency reasons, but government failure in the regulatory process has come under close scrutiny. A broad overview of the policy issues and some basic aspects of efficient transport policies are given in ECMT (1994*a*) and summarised in Box 1.

Distorted relative prices make rational decision making difficult

Achieving a set of optimal prices (prices equalling marginal social costs) is a difficult task because charging for infrastructure is sometimes difficult and the assignment of monetary values to environmental, congestion and security costs is fraught with uncertainties. Despite the introduction of a toll system on motorways in 1955, it has only recently been used as a traffic management tool, pricing

Box 1. Efficiency aspects of transport policies

Infrastructure policy. Transport infrastructure provides capacity (traffic lanes, runways or railway lines), as well as durability (thickness of pavement). If infrastructure is unpriced, users ignore their contribution to congestion and infrastructure wear in their travel decisions with the result that the social costs of transport exceed private costs. In principle, the user and not the taxpayer should pay the full cost of the trip, and the authorities should set congestion and infrastructure wear charges to close this gap (pricing rule). An optimal amount of investment will be achieved, if capacity and durability are produced to the point where the marginal social benefits from raising investment in each dimension equals marginal social cost (investment rule). The pricing and investment rules constitute an efficient long-run policy, in which a user's full marginal cost is determined at the right level of capacity and durability (Winston, 1991). Correct pricing is a prerequisite for making efficient infrastructure investment. If the returns to capacity and durability are constant, marginal cost pricing will fully cover capital and operating costs. Decreasing returns will lead to deficits and increasing returns to excess revenues.

Natural monopolies. If economies of scale are important, competition could quickly lead to the elimination of competitors, leaving only a monopoly. This is likely to occur in the rail sector and has led to stringent regulation or nationalisation of rail companies in most OECD countries. The importance of natural monopoly has probably declined due to technical progress and inter-modal competition. Natural monopoly arguments may also only apply to infrastructure, but not to service provision.

Environmental externalities. Most transport modes generate environmental externalities in the form of air pollution, noise and land use, but agents lack incentives to take the cost of environmental degradation into account. Such external costs should be internalised, for instance, by allocating property rights or setting a tax at the level where the cost of additional abatement just outweighs the gains from reduced emissions. In some cases, taxation of a pollutant may be difficult and a regulatory approach preferred.

Public or private infrastructure provision. Where charging systems are difficult to devise, such as for local roads, provision will need to be public. In addition, long gestation periods, break-even points far in the future, indivisibility and irreversibility imply a high risk to private investors, which is probably why so few large infrastructure projects are undertaken on a private basis.

Government failure. The traditional theory of regulation takes for granted that policies serve the public interest by correcting some form of market failure. The weakness of this view is that social welfare maximisation is rarely the sole criterion for managing the regulation or running a regulated firm. For several reasons, regulation can create, not eliminate, inefficiencies (Winston, 1993). For example, well-organised groups will tend to benefit more from regulation, than broad, diffuse ones and the regulator will seek to preserve a politically optimal distribution of rents across the coalition of well-organised groups. In addition, asymmetric information between the regulator and regulated could lead to badly designed intervention and regulatory constraints could lead to a provision of services which fails to significantly minimise costs. These problems are in addition to the direct costs imposed by regulation.

being largely geared towards achieving long-term balanced budget objectives. In general, this seems to be possible, but does not lead to efficient management, as rents on profitable parts of the motorway sector are increasingly used to build unprofitable ones. For the rail sector budget balancing has also been the most important objective, but one which has been seldom achieved, despite considerable State support.

Until the mid-1980s virtually all transport service prices were fixed not only to reduce intra-modal competition, but also to protect the highest cost inter-modal competitor. The system was supplemented by quotas and other access restrictions, but has evolved rapidly since then, largely reflecting EU-wide moves towards liberalisation (Table 24). Road pricing was freed in the mid-1980s, resulting in large market share losses for the rail freight business, although the prices of the latter were freed at the same time. Airline prices were freed, in several stages, by 1991. More recently, the SNCF has obtained additional freedom in setting prices for passenger services (which were, in general, uniform and depended on kilometres travelled), and the setting of road tolls has become more liberal. The few experiments which exist show that varying road tolls with traffic density has a considerable impact on traffic flows. Price liberalisation has certainly brought the transport sector closer to achieving economic efficiency. However, further progress could be made in several areas. Infrastructure costs are not fully imputed for road freight services, which has a counterpart in an infrastructure subsidy for the SNCF. In addition, environmental and congestion costs are seldom included, even though the subject is discussed with fervour. For example, a relatively low diesel tax favours trucking.

All large rail and road projects are evaluated according to criteria laid down in the Act on Inland Transport. However, these criteria are rather vaguely defined and procedures differ for road and rail projects. The SNCF provides an indicator for financial and overall benefits, the latter adding changes in producer surplus on other modes of transport and consumer surplus to changes in the SNCF's profitability. The assessment of motorway projects takes a broader approach and, as well as financial rate of return, includes environmental, employment or regional impacts. The latter are clearly difficult to quantify and compare across projects. Apart from these differences, uncertainties surround many of the parameters and projected values of such calculations. These concern, for instance, projected traffic growth, effects on other modes, future relative prices or the monetisation

Table 24. **Transport sector policies: an overview**

	Road		Urban public transport (Paris)	Rail		Air	
	Freight	Passengers		Freight	Passengers	International	Domestic
Access	liberal	partly open	closed	closed	closed	liberal	partly open
Pricing	free	partly free	fixed	free	partly free	free	largely free
Competition							
Intra-modal	strong	medium	non existent	non existent	non existent	strong	weak
Inter-modal	weak	weak	weak	strong	strong	weak	weak[1]
Ownership	private	private	public	public	public	largely public	largely public
Labour standards	flexible	flexible	very rigid	very rigid	very rigid	rigid	rigid

1. Strong on a few routes.
Source: OECD.

81

of time gained or improved comfort for consumers of transport services. In the past, projections of rates of return by the Transport Ministry have been much more optimistic than those by the Finance Ministry. In principle, projects should show a rate of return of more than 8 per cent. A working group of the *Commissariat Général du Plan* (*Rapport Boiteux*, 1994) has recently suggested that the evaluation of projects be standardised as far as possible[65] and verified by an independent agency. In practice, economic and financial considerations are often overtaken in the decision-making process by other considerations. Both the RATP and the SNCF, for instance, have recently started loss-making projects linking the east and west of Paris, and the Rhine-Rhône canal project shows a negative rate of return.

Liberalisation has led to adjustment problems

The liberalisation of the transport sector has raised intra-modal and inter-modal competition significantly (Table 24). However, the speed of adjustment across sectors has differed considerably and led to severe problems in some of them. The road freight sector has probably adjusted the best so far, while the SNCF, which had already faced the problem of reducing its workforce over previous decades, is finding it difficult to accelerate the pace of restructuring. Change is especially slow at public airlines and the Parisian urban transport system.[66] Slow adjustment comes at a considerable cost to the public, state assistance amounting to about FF 50 billion in 1994.

Several factors are important in explaining why the process appears painful, slow and costly. It is a widely held view that market forces in the transport sector should play a role only at the margin, while the State should continue to guide developments (*déréglementation maîtrisée*) and that liberalisation could lead to too much competition (*concurrence destructrice*), producers and their employees needing protection. Protected sectors, and especially their unions, also embrace such views and the unions make them heard. Every single transport sector has had at least one major strike in the last ten years (with the RATP recording strikes twice a week). In the aftermath of these strikes reform projects are usually withdrawn or significantly watered down and the strike experience has clearly reduced the zeal of politicians for pushing ahead with necessary reforms. Adjustment is also made difficult by extremely rigid work practices in public transport enterprises and the fact that dismissals are possible *de jure*, but impossible *de facto*.

Regional considerations strongly influence policy decisions

While all large infrastructure projects are subject to a financial and socio-economic cost-benefit analysis, regional policy objectives have gained considerable importance in final investment decisions, in the drawing-up of national master plans and as an argument for keeping unprofitable services running. Several aspects of the interface between transport and regional policies are shaping the current debate: *i)* regional income distribution in France is one of the most uneven in the OECD (Cingolani, 1993), making regional equity issues an important political topic, *ii)* equity considerations (accessibility or the right to transport at a "fair" price) are often invoked as a justification for investing in loss-making projects or continuing unprofitable services, *iii)* most important, perhaps, improved transport services are seen as boosting the growth of lagging regions in a way that market-driven adjustment cannot achieve.

Large inter-regional income differences exist in some OECD Member countries and the causes of their persistence are not always well understood. Recent research stresses the advantages of large agglomerations in terms of achieving scale economies and procuring positive externalities, which outweigh higher wages and prices and negative externalities. Lower transport costs could favour regional polarisation, as the costs of serving regions from an economically advantageous agglomeration fall. On the other hand, transport infrastructure could open new markets to lagging regions and lower costs could give an incentive to locate there (ECMT, 1994*b*). Such an incentive might be small in France, however, as the minimum wage is no longer regionally differentiated.

The cost of regional policies appears to be rising rapidly. The SNCF, for example, cannot cut unprofitable lines or replace existing services with lower-cost transport modes, although this situation could improve with the new regionalisation programme. Furthermore, a socio-economic rate of return of 8 per cent is seldom reached for investment going to low-density regions. The TGV[67] *Est* project, for example, is only being built with the help of a large subsidy and the Rhine-Rhône canal project will be highly unprofitable. In the future many regional cities will be served simultaneously by subsidised highways, railways and airline services. As these services compete with each other, project profitability is reduced further. In addition, the cross-subsidisation of services weakens the financial performance of public enterprises and, to the degree that it causes prices to diverge from full social costs, stimulates inefficient over or under consumption of the affected services.

There is no evidence supporting the notion that a large amount of under-utilised transport infrastructure is helpful in boosting the growth of lagging regions and *ex post* evaluation of the regional impacts of infrastructure projects is virtually non-existent.[68] As argued above, it could even run counter to regional equity objectives and the additional tax burden may reduce overall growth. Other policy instruments, such as lower taxation in lagging regions or a regional differentiation of the minimum wage, might be more effective in achieving regional policy objectives.

Public transport spending and revenues

France is pursuing a medium-term fiscal policy programme aimed at a reduction in net borrowing and expenditure restraint. The expenditure restraint target is very stringent as it aims at no real increase in overall outlays, implying a fall in primary expenditure (excluding interest payments) in real terms. While government spending on the transport sector is not of a sufficient size to have a strong impact on the future course of overall spending, lower expenditure and higher revenues would no doubt be helpful in achieving medium-term commitments.

Future infrastructure investment is likely to be considerable, even though many projects will be viable only with public financial support. More rational pricing should lead to a better use of existing facilities and, in combination with a scaling back of the regional policy component, future outlays could be reduced substantially. Spending could also be reduced by the speeding up of structural adjustment of publicly-owned enterprises and their privatisation could reduce public debt. Finally, revenues could be raised, for instance, by increasing the diesel tax or by charging higher tolls on heavily travelled motorway sections.

Sectoral developments and policy issues

Road transport

Infrastructure investment

Relative to population the French road network is among the most extensive in the OECD (Table 25). Traffic is heavy along the North-South axis from Lille to Marseille. The motorway network has been expanding rapidly over the last 25 years and is, at present, the third longest in the world after the United States and Germany. Most motorways are toll-roads (OECD, 1987),[69] the toll system having been introduced as early as 1955. The State grants concessions and determines technical construction characteristics, toll rates (to a certain extent) and supervises network operation.[70] Initially, concessions were granted to companies of a mixed public and private character (*Sociétés d'économie mixte*, SEMS)[71] and to four private groups during the early 1970s.

In the early 1980s, the financial situation of the private companies started to deteriorate and the Government took over three loss-making private holdings and turned them into SEMS. At the same time, policy changed from a project to a network-oriented approach. The initial notion of financial equilibrium per concession-holding company has altered towards one aiming at financial equilibrium at the motorway-industry level. As a result of this changed approach, variations in toll rates fell considerably over the 1980s. Despite the good profits generated by some SEMS, the long-term debts of all motorway companies rose to FF 99 billion in 1993. Recently, the six biggest companies were regrouped into three major companies. Cofiroute, the only remaining private company, was unaffected. The purpose of the reform was to ensure the continuation of the prevailing system of cross subsidisation, the bigger companies with their relatively high capacity for raising capital taking over heavily-indebted smaller firms. The new structure will sustain the continuation of an ambitious motorway extension programme: 2 600 kilometres are to be built over the next 10 years, increasing the current network by more than one-third. In the main these projects will be unprofitable and built for regional policy reasons. Part of the new motorways will not be toll-roads, as traffic density is unlikely to cover the cost of collecting tolls using current technology.

Although motorway tolls differ, they are far from complying with the rules of efficient pricing.[72] In principle, tolls should be related to investment outlays,

Table 25. International road comparison

	France		Germany		United Kingdom		Italy	
	1980	1991	1980	1991	1980	1991	1980	1991
Network length (km)	489 000	491 700	479 521	501 000	339 633	386 546	296 270	305 067
of which: motorways	4 801	7 080	8 967	10 854	2 556	3 259	5 900	6 214
Passenger cars (including taxis) (thousands)[1]	19 130	23 810	23 192	31 322	15 629	21 515[2]	17 686	27 120
Number of lorries (thousands)[1]	2 515	3 685	1 277	1 440	1 736	2 348[2]	n.a.	n.a.
of which: load capacity 10 000 kg and over	66.7	64.0	61.8[3]	89.1	112.9	272.5	n.a.	n.a.
Number of private cars per 1000 inhabitants		413		480		361		478
Killed in traffic accidents[4]		10 028		6 875		5 262[2]		n.a.
of which: car drivers and passengers		6 437		4 250		2 206		n.a.
Killed in traffic accidents related to population (× 1000)[1]		0.18		0.11		0.10[2]		n.a.

1. Data pertain to West Germany.
2. Data pertain to Great Britain only.
3. No data available on lorries with load capacity exceeding 15 000 kg.
4. 1987 data.
Source: UN, OECD, ECMT, Observatoire de l'automobile.

which have two dimensions: they raise capacity (reduce congestion) and affect durability (wear and tear). If users are only charged for part of these cost components, excess demand and high repair costs will prevail. The implementation of efficient pricing practices – prices dependent on distance travelled, congestion, weight, number of axles – could reduce future capital spending and improve the condition and efficiency of roads. Congestion costs in France are estimated at 2 per cent of GDP (Quinet, 1994), although a complete elimination of congestion would not be optimal. Recent experiments allowing for wider variations in tolls show that price variations have a considerable influence on traffic flows: on the A1 motorway peak-load pricing has reduced traffic by 13 to 15 per cent during the weekend rush-hours and vouchers are given to travellers in the summer to encourage them to use motorways surrounding the Paris region. This offer was taken up by more than 80 per cent of travellers in 1993.

Investment priority has been given to the expansion of the motorway network, even though the upgrading of trunkroads to dual carriageways would often be cheaper.[73] This is because financing is easier for motorway expansion as the budgeting process is avoided and financing from profitable motorway companies is available. Also planning periods are much longer for the national network than for motorways (Vornetti, 1994). Infrastructural road and motorway investment amounted to FF 58 billion in 1994. This included FF 14 billion for motorways, almost all of which was financed by the motorway companies (Table 26).

Table 26. **Infrastructure investment**
FF billion, 1994

	State	Local government	Other	Total
Roads	7.5	35.9	..	43.4
Motorways	0.0	0.0	14.1	14.1
Urban transport[1]	1.6	4.8	4.3	10.7
SNCF	0.4	1.8	7.8	10.0
Ports	0.2	0.6	2.0	2.8
Airports	1.2	0.1	2.0	3.3
Total	10.9	43.2	30.2	84.3
As a per cent of GDP	0.1	0.6	0.4	1.1

1. Including urban transport services by the SNCF.
Source: OEST.

Individual transport

Individual road passenger transport[74] is significant in terms of passenger-kilometres, but only a small part is carried out commercially (Figure 14). Since 1970, the number of private cars and passenger-kilometres travelled has increased markedly.

Accounting for road infrastructure costs and road related fiscal receipts is not simple: there are difficulties in splitting road expenditure between private vehicles and trucks, and it is not clear whether excise taxes only should enter such a calculation, or whether value added taxes should also be included. However, irrespective of the method of calculation, revenue from taxes levied on private car use is sizeable, largely reflecting the high rate of tax on gasoline,

Figure 14. **DOMESTIC PASSENGER TRAFFIC**

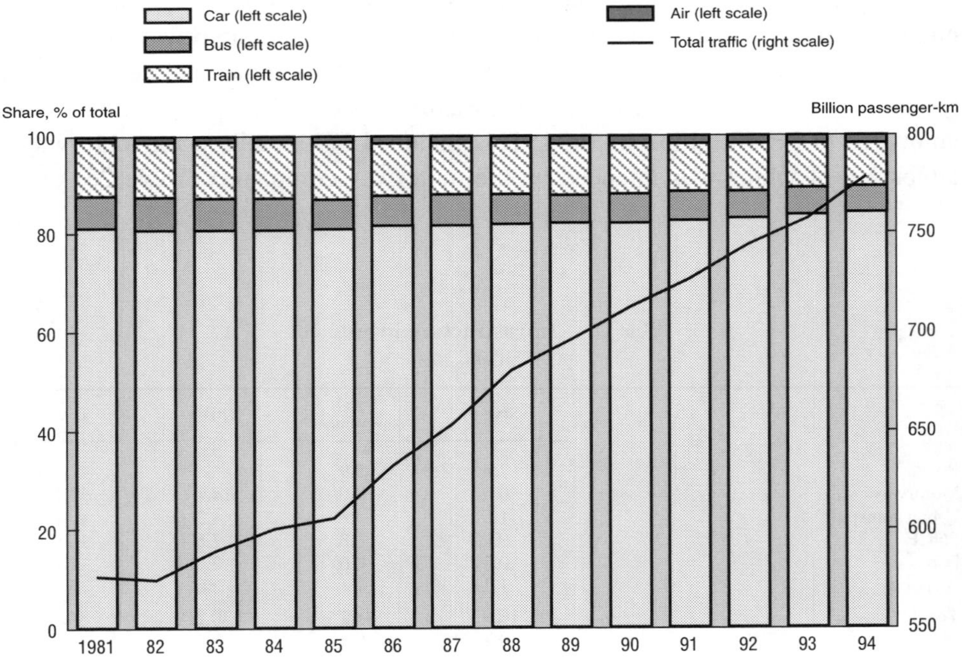
Car (left scale)
Bus (left scale)
Train (left scale)
Air (left scale)
Total traffic (right scale)
Share, % of total
Billion passenger-km
100
80
60
40
20
0
800
750
700
650
600
550
1981
82
83
84
85
86
87
88
89
90
91
92
93
94

Source: OEST.

which is among the highest in the OECD (Figure 15). Excise taxes on diesel are much lower and have changed little in recent years, while the real price of diesel has fallen even more than that of gasoline since the early 1980s. Tax receipts on the acquisition and utilisation of private cars clearly exceed imputed infrastructural outlays by a wide margin (OEST, 1994). Whether they also cover social costs is more difficult to say (see below).

Transport by bus is not very important, its market share falling steadily over time. While there are no access and pricing restrictions for the tourist bus service industry, the development of scheduled bus services is severely hampered by regulatory measures. For instance, buses can only use highways with the permission of the regional administration, which is usually not granted as it would often make unprofitable train services along the same route even more unprofitable. However, replacing unprofitable train services by buses would in many cases be economic and increase service flexibility considerably. For example, deregulation of scheduled services in the United Kingdom in the early 1980s led to a substantial fall in the real prices of bus trips and a considerable rise in bus traffic, without endangering road safety.[75]

Road haulage

The majority of freight is transported by road (Figure 16). The number of trucks has been increasing continuously and with it the number of vehicle-kilometres, and the share of trucking in total freight transport rose sharply from 48 per cent in 1983 to 61 per cent in 1993. Road haulage has certain characteristics which enhance its competitive edge *vis-à-vis* other modes of transport. The capacity to transport door to door is almost unlimited, whereas alternative transport modes are restricted by the limited scale of their networks. Other major advantages are flexibility as regards time, relative speed and the variability with which quantities can be delivered. Another important factor underlying the growth of road haulage is the decline in relative prices resulting from: greater competitive pressures following significant liberalisation, falling oil prices in the mid-1980s, and the fact that negative externalities are not reflected in service prices.

Quantitative restrictions on short-distance road haulage were phased out at the beginning of the 1980s. On the other hand, until the 1986 reform, long-distance road haulage was regulated by a system consisting of quotas[76] and

Figure 15. AUTOMOTIVE FUEL PRICES AND TAXES

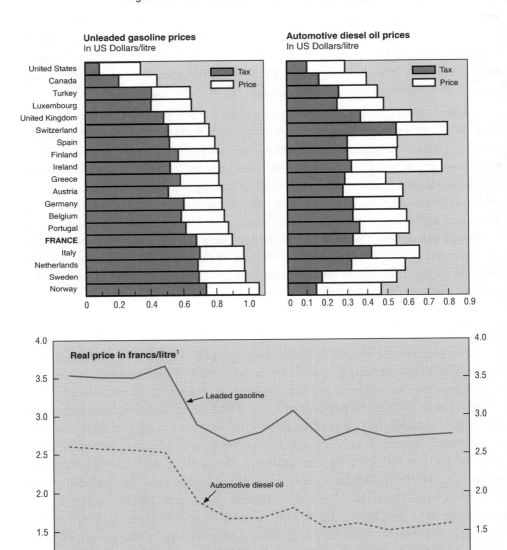

1. In constant 1980 prices; adjusted by the GDP deflator.
Source: IEA, *Energy Prices and Taxes.*

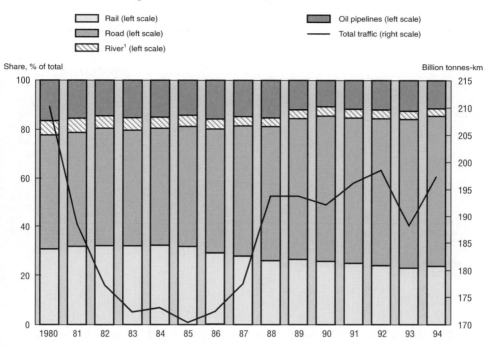

Figure 16. **DOMESTIC FREIGHT TRANSPORT**

Rail (left scale)

Road (left scale)

River[1] (left scale)

Oil pipelines (left scale)

Total traffic (right scale)

Share, % of total

Billion tonnes-km

1. Rhine traffic excluded from 1982 onwards.
Source: OEST.

regulated prices, which was largely designed to protect the railways from competition. Quantitative restrictions were phased out between 1986 and 1990. The obligatory road transport rate (introduced in 1961) was replaced in 1987 by an indicative road transport rate for certain categories of freight. However, the indicative rates have never been an effective instrument for regulating prices. The liberalisation of prices and freeing of access has contributed to a considerable decline in road transport rates (Figure 17), some squeeze on profits and a sharp gain in market share. Complementing the deregulation of road transport, the French competition authorities have played an active role in ensuring that the benefits from liberalisation do in fact materialise. For example, in June 1988 the Competition Council condemned concerted practices between the French National Federation of Freight Forwarders and the main transport firms and imposed heavy fines on the parties (OECD, 1990).

Figure 17. **RELATIVE TRANSPORT PRICES**[1]

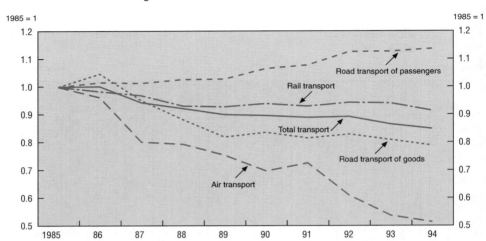

1985 = 1

1985 = 1

Competition will increase further with continuing European-wide deregulation. Cabotage began in 1990, initially under quota restrictions, but these quotas will continue to rise until complete liberalisation is achieved in July 1998. In the absence of good competitiveness indicators,[77] it is difficult to judge the effects of further European-wide moves towards liberalisation on the French road haulage industry. In the member states of the EU there are significant differences in the cost structures of road haulage that are largely due to different tax-regimes, social legislation and wage costs. Where the latter are concerned, Greek, Spanish and Portuguese road hauliers should have a significant competitive advantage.

Road haulage generates considerable costs due to the significant contribution of trucks to the wear and tear on roads, substantial congestion costs, particularly in urban areas, relatively high energy consumption, sizeable negative environmental externalities and safety costs. In contrast to private vehicles, fiscal receipts do not cover infrastructure outlays. According to OEST (1994) calculations, they cover less than half of government outlays – diesel is relatively lightly taxed and even though tolls on lorries are higher in principle, in practice they come close to passenger car tolls for lorries with a subscription. Such an average calculation for all trucks and all roads covers a wide range of situations: for instance, a heavy truck driving on an uncongested motorway covers more than the infrastructure and social costs.

Safety and environmental issues

Car and truck use leads to sizeable negative externalities in the form of accidents and air and noise pollution, which are considerably higher than for other modes of transport (Figure 18). Estimates of overall environmental costs vary between FF 110 billion (INFRAS/IWW, 1995) and FF 130 billion (Merlin, 1994) per year. When the cost of accidents is included, the INFRAS/IWW estimate rises to FF 258 billion or 4½ per cent of GDP.[78] Per unit of output, external costs are by far the highest for trucks. On an international comparison, external costs are especially high for trucks, due to the high accident rate and low load factors in France. On the other hand, they are very low for railways, reflecting the low accident rate, extensive electrification and the large share of nuclear energy in electricity output.

Speed limits are often ignored by truck drivers, as transport firms are under pressure from forwarding agents for quick delivery. In order to improve road safety the Government introduced a system of penalty points, which can lead to the withdrawing of a driver's license. It triggered a massive strike in 1992. While deregulation has certainly not raised incentives to respect legislation, the number of violations in the early 1990s was little different from that in the early 1980s, before deregulation. Incentives to respect the speed and hours worked limits could be raised by stricter and more frequent controls and higher fines for infringements, both of which appear to be relatively low on an international comparison. A law adopted in early 1995 should improve the situation in this respect.

The cost of externalities exceeds the financial contributions of road hauliers. It would be wrong, however, to use total damage per unit as a benchmark for an optimum rate of internalisation. The latter crucially depends on the steepness of the abatement cost curve for the different transport modes. An official assessment of all social costs argues for an overall increase in diesel taxes of FF 1.7 per litre (which would raise the price, excluding VAT, by 53 per cent). It would raise an estimated FF 44 billion per year.[79] It would clearly be beneficial in terms of

Figure 18. **RELATIVE EXTERNAL COSTS OF TRANSPORT**[1]

1991

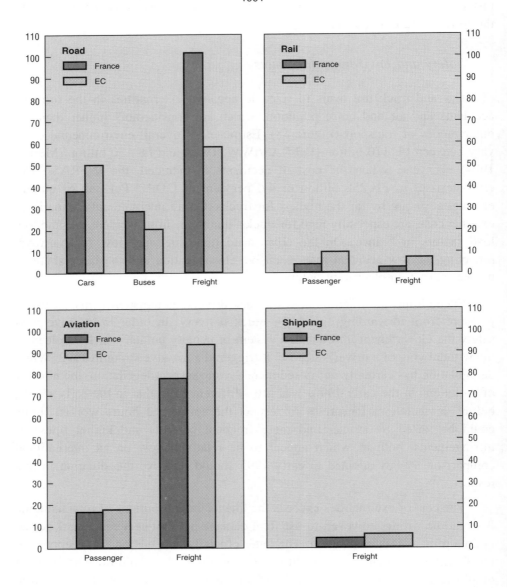

1. ECU per 1 000 passenger kilometres for passenger transport and per 1 000 tonnes kilometres for freight transport.
Source: INFRAS/IWW (1995).

lowering pollution and raising safety, in improving the competitive position of the rail sector, and in raising government income in a non-distortionary fashion.

Rail transport

Overall demand for rail transport services has suffered a trend decline, with both rail passenger transport on the classical network and rail goods transport diminishing significantly. In particular, the competitive position of goods transport by rail relative to other modes of transport has deteriorated markedly. On the other hand, the development of the high speed train (TGV) has been commercially viable so far. The structural decline in demand and the substantial outlays on infrastructure have led to a deterioration in the financial position of the SNCF, despite substantial financial contributions by the State. In spite of difficulties in raising the pace of structural adjustment and a deteriorating financial position, the French rail transport sector is still among the more efficient in Europe (Figure 19). The SNCF's market share of passenger and freight transport is still relatively high and productivity levels compare well with those in the other large European countries. In addition, financial results (including government support) are generally better than elsewhere. Excluding government support, the revenue/cost ratio was about average in the late 1980s, but significantly lower than in Japan, the United Kingdom or Sweden. Controlling for many exogenous variables, such as trip length or load factors, Oum and Yu (1994) also provide evidence that the SNCF is among the better performing rail companies OECD-wide – albeit that there are not many good performers in the field. The study also shows that a low level of subsidisation and large degree of managerial autonomy improves performance in general.

The infrastructure

The French rail network is among the most extensive in the OECD. The length of the classical network (*réseau classique, i.e.* excluding the TGV) has remained stable over the last 15 years,[80] while the TGV network has expanded rapidly (see Box 2).

Freight and passenger transport services

As noted in Box 2, the number of passengers travelling on TGV's has risen substantially. In sharp contrast, the number of passenger-kilometres on the classical network has decreased by nearly a third. Econometric estimates (in a submis-

Figure 19. **RAILWAY COMPANY PERFORMANCE**

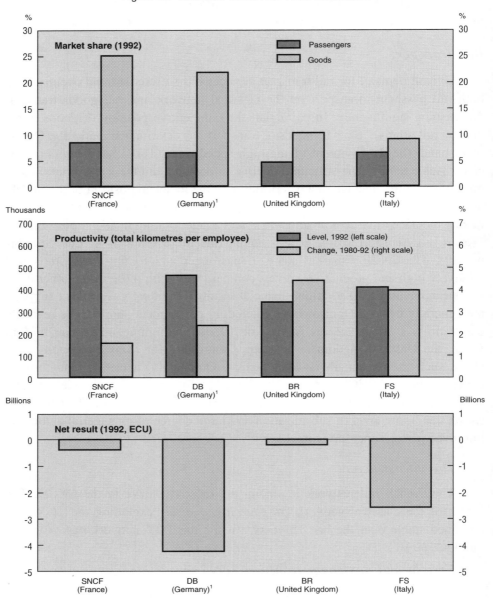

1. Western Germany except for the market share of goods.
Source: SNCF (1994), *Réseaux ferroviaires européens, comparaison internationale.*

Box 2. The development of the TGV network

The introduction of high-speed trains demonstrates the capacity of rail companies to innovate and has improved the quality of rail services by cutting travelling times considerably. Since it was introduced in France in 1981, TGV passenger traffic has risen steadily, to 19 billion passenger kilometres in 1993 or 39 per cent of the total. It is a serious alternative to short-distance flights and has reinforced inter-modal competition on some routes. Pricing is liberal on most lines. The development of the present TGV network required sizeable investment, and outlays on infrastructure increased steadily during the second part of the 1980s, reaching a peak of close to FF 9 billion in 1991.

The profitability of TGV projects crucially depends on traffic density and investment cost. The earliest project incurred an infrastructural cost of FF 26 million per kilometre, whereas it will be about FF 200 million for the planned Lyon-Turin line. So far, projects have been built along the busiest routes, some of which already suffered from capacity constraints, at relatively low investment cost. They have shown a financial profitability of 14 per cent, far above the reference rate of 8 per cent and, including externalities, social rates of return are even higher. As investment costs have become higher, passenger density lower and competition against the existing rapid train network stronger, the profitability of projects has fallen and most new TGV projects are likely to show a rate of return of only 5½ per cent, well below the reference rate. A large part of the infrastructural cost of future projects will be paid by the State and the regions, assistance being provided for regional development reasons. Such future subsidies could be substantial. In the case of the Paris-Strasbourg project, for example, they could amount to FF 13 billion, half the estimated project cost.

sion by the French administration) show that total rail passenger transport grew only at about half the rate of aggregate consumption and faces rather stiff competition from road transport (the price elasticity being somewhat below 1).[81]

The demand for rail freight transport was already suffering from the structural weakness of major client branches and it fell further following road-haulage deregulation in the mid-1980s. Rail freight prices have also declined (they are not published), but presumably to a lesser extent than those in the road sector. The SNCF has reacted to the drop in freight transport by reducing the number of freight-stations by 50 per cent over the last 10 years. While reducing costs, fewer freight stations lowers flexibility. Transport by single wagon (*lotissement*), which is largely unprofitable, has diminished most. However, there are still 20 000 employees in this sector and, given social constraints, a rapid reduction in their number is impossible. More rapid growth in combined rail/road transport has been too small to offset overall market-share losses. The development of a "rail motorway"[82] could trigger significant growth in this sector and have considerable advantages over road transport in terms of limiting environmental cost, improving safety and saving energy. Its development would, however, entail a considerable amount of investment and the socio-economic profitability would be far below 8 per cent.

Financial considerations

Despite reducing its workforce (from 253 000 in 1982 to 192 000 in 1993)[83] and realising productivity gains of about $1\frac{1}{2}$ per cent per year over the last decade, the financial position of the SNCF has weakened and indebtedness is considerable. The SNCF's statute states that it should aim at balance sheet equilibrium, but, despite substantial contributions from the State over the last 10 years, it was only attained between 1989 and 1991, followed by significant losses, particularly since 1993, because of the fall in traffic and inadequate cost controls (Table 27). As its charter includes the obligation to provide certain unprofitable passenger services, it would seem difficult to achieve financial equilibrium without state and regional contributions. Such assistance is intended for the maintenance of structurally unprofitable lines[84] (FF 4 billion in 1994) and compensation for state-imposed price reductions (FF 7 billion).

Three additional factors are responsible for the sizeable public contributions to SNCF (a budgeted FF 48 billion in 1994 overall): *i)* the French State underwrites infrastructure outlays (FF 12 billion), *ii)* the heavy investment programme during the 1980s led to a rapid debt accumulation and a sharp rise in interest payments, of which FF 4 billion are paid by the State, and *iii)* SNCF employees are not in the general social security pension scheme, but covered by the SNCF's own pension system. Given unfavourable demographic trends and generous pensions,[85] public contributions to the pension scheme amount to FF 15 billion.[86] Despite this substantial subsidisation, the debt of the SNCF reached $2\frac{1}{2}$ per cent of GDP in 1994.

Reform of railway services

Responsibility for regional passenger services could soon be passed to the regions, in order to improve incentives to streamline loss-making regional ser-

Table 27. **The SNCF: result by activity and public contributions**

FF million

	1990	1991	1992	1993	1994[1]
A. Result by activity					
Passenger and freight	3 168	2 011	1 176	−1 286	−664
Passengers					
of which:					
Rapid express	3 358	2 581	3 025	1 479	697
Regional services	−129	−290	−886	−1 184	−1 284
Freight	−60	−280	−963	−1 518	−1 361
Infrastructure	−4 308	−4 466	−4 782	−8 019	−8 324
Exceptional	1 156	2 461	651	1 597	2 088
Total SNCF	17	6	−2 956	−8 396	−8 598
B. State contribution towards the SNCF[2]					
Social tariffs	3 405	3 434	3 015	3 852	3 672
Infrastructural outlays	10 432	10 765	11 714	11 696	11 857
Regional services	3 887	3 911	4 008	4 162	4 298
Other	5 032	1 088	574	609	756
Total contribution towards operating costs	22 756	19 198	19 911	20 319	20 583
Pensions	14 118	14 432	14 705	13 118	13 182
Debt rescheduling	..	4 039	4 140	4 273	4 282
Total	36 774	37 669	38 756	37 573	38 047

1.   Estimates.
2.   Excluding the Parisian suburbs.
Source: SNCF.

vices. A new scheme started in October 1994 on an experimental basis and nine regions are participating in it. In order to participate, regions have to draw up transport policy plans, define transport objectives and sign a service agreement with the SNCF. As soon as the contract between the State and the SNCF for 1996-2000 is signed, the system could come officially into force. Before then, agreement needs to be reached on how the State's subsidy for loss-making services will be shared between the regions.

The sharp deterioration in the financial position of the SNCF shows that structural change is too slow. This can be attributed to two factors:

– The SNCF's legal statute heavily constrains its commercial freedom. It has freedom of pricing only for freight services and most TGV lines and has virtually no power to close unprofitable services and lines. Cuts in the network, for instance, can be vetoed by local authorities. Regionalisation of services may help in this respect.

–   Work practices are very rigid (the general work legislation does not apply) and attempts at restructuring are usually blocked by strong social constraints.

Little commercial freedom, very stringent security and rigid labour standards make it difficult for the SNCF to compete against other modes of transport, which operate under much more liberal conditions. There are currently no plans to address any of these issues.

Reforms, however, appear urgent. Projections by the SNCF show that, given the already high debt levels and an ambitious investment programme, the deficit (even with subsidies at the current level) will reach FF 13.5 billion[87] by 2000 and stabilise thereafter. This would lead to a debt explosion, with debt rising to FF 400 billion in 2005 (about four times the turnover). In addition, EU-wide liberalisation of rail services has started, and the SNCF could lose in competitiveness to countries that move faster in terms of liberalising their rail services. So far, access has been opened up only for combined transport services and the transit of trains, the EU aiming in a first instance at separating the accounting of infrastructure from services (institutional separation is optional). If current reforms in other countries are successful (ECMT, 1993), pressure to move further in liberalising provision of other services could strengthen (Box 3).

Urban transport

Given its diversity, it is impossible to review urban transport policies in detail, and the *Ile de France* region, which is one of the most important European agglomerations, serves here as an example.[88] Despite an increase in public transport, the region suffers from congestion and rising environmental problems, but preference for private car use remains strong. Automobile use has already been made more onerous and costly in recent years (by reducing the available amount of parking space, making parking more expensive, providing express lanes for buses, extending pedestrian zones etc.). While these measures may have slowed the rise in private car use, they have not reduced it. Therefore, additional measures might be required, *e.g.* the introduction of tolls on urban roads (*péage urbain*), at least on a trial-basis (STP, 1991).[89]

The SNCF and the RATP provide most public transport in the *Ile de France* through four modes: the *Métro*, the bus, suburban trains, and the RER (*Réseau*

Box 3. **Reforms of rail companies**

In order to improve the performance of their rail companies, several countries have changed the regulatory environment, and in the cases of New Zealand and the United Kingdom privatised them. The reform of British Rail appears to be the most radical. After significant restructuring along geographical and organisational lines during the 1980s, privatisation is now underway. Activities are being split into different companies: Rail-track, which is supervised by a government agency, controls the infrastructure and charges users for the use of the network. Freight transport is being completely privatised and opened to competition. Passenger transport services, which are in deficit, will continue to receive government subsidies, but will be conceded to private operators.

After a bad financial performance for 20 years, the Japanese Government corporatised Japan National Railways in 1987. Six publicly-owned regional passenger transport companies and one freight transport company were created. Each of these owns its own network and the debt of the earlier enterprise was largely taken over by the Government. In contrast to the United Kingdom, service competition is not envisaged. Since 1987, many unprofitable lines have been closed, overstaffing reduced significantly, and productivity and profitability have received a significant boost (OECD, 1992*b*).

As in the United Kingdom, network and service provision were separated in Sweden in 1988. The two companies have remained public, however, and service provision is not open to competition on the major freight and passenger lines. Regional lines have become the responsibility of a regional administrative body and regional concessions are open to competition, although only one private operator has entered the market since 1990.

The railway system in Germany is also in the course of being restructured. The *Bundesbahn* and the *Reichsbahn* have been merged to form *Deutsche Bahn AG*, and a large amount of debt been taken over by the Government. The new organisation has been split into regulatory and entrepreneurial entities. Commercial activities have been further split into passenger, freight and network departments, which – with the exception of the latter – will be privatised separately later on. Regional lines have become the responsibility of the regional authorities. *Deutsche Bahn AG* showed a sharp productivity rise and made a profit in 1994.

In New Zealand, the rail industry, excluding the land under the tracks, has been privatised. Only intra-city and suburban services are subsidised and the company is profitable.

In the United States, passenger services are of little importance, but rail freight, on the other hand, has a significant market share. Virtually all freight rail companies are private and own their tracks, and the sector is profitable, despite strong inter-modal competition. Regulation of rail freight companies is very light.

express régional – a regional rail network). Public transport is heavily subsidised and tariffs are much lower than in other French cities and most metropolises around the world, particularly when compared with London or New York. The price of *Métro* tickets is not dependent on the length of the trip[90] and passengers contribute only about 40 per cent to total transport receipts. A transport tax (paid by employers) contributes 16 per cent to the receipts of the RATP and 36 per cent to SNCF services in the suburbs of Paris. In addition, the State and the region provide an additional FF 6 billion to the RATP and FF 1 billion to the SNCF. These arrangements are unique to the Paris region. The State sets the price for public urban transport in Paris at a level far below cost, revenue shortfalls being automatically covered by public funds. As a consequence the RATP has little incentive to improve its performance and strive for budget equilibrium.[91] User fees are scheduled to rise from the current 40 per cent cost coverage rate to 50 per cent by the year 2000, through an increase in fares higher than the inflation rate.[92] The development of suburban centres with relatively low population densities – a difficult environment in which to develop urban transport – has dampened the rise in traffic, which has stagnated since the early 1980s.

Like the SNCF, the RATP is heavily debt-burdened due to high investment outlays. Furthermore, labour costs amount to roughly two-thirds of exploitation costs: the average wage level is higher in the RATP than in road-haulage and in the overall urban transport sector (Merlin, 1994). In addition, the pension scheme is similar to that of the SNCF (see above) and is again much more generous than private sector schemes. Work practices are also extremely rigid and the level of strike activity very high.[93] Partly reflecting strong social constraints, there are no reform projects either to pull labour standards into line with the private sector or to privatise part of the services (for example, bus services).[94] On the other hand, there have been several reform projects to hand over responsibility to the *Ile de France* region, which would have ended subsidisation of regional Parisian transport out of the State's budget.

Air transport

With an increase in volume of 6 per cent per year during the 1980s, air transport is a high growth industry. However, strengthening competition from charter flights and successive EU-wide liberalisation packages have harmed the profitability of most scheduled airlines in Europe. Most hurt were airlines with high costs that were slow to adjust to a more competition-oriented environment. The difficulties were compounded by falling business during the last recession, when Air France incurred staggering losses. Restructuring of domestic scheduled flights is in its early stages and they will become completely liberalised only in 1997. On the other hand, the profitability of charter carriers with relatively low operating costs has been fairly good.

The major part of French air transport is conducted by the state-owned *Compagnie nationale Air France* (CNAF), which is the outcome of a merger in 1992 between Air France and UTA (*Union des transports aériens*). Through the merger CNAF obtained a 75 per cent stake in Air Inter. Air France serves international destinations and Air Inter largely domestic ones. Apart from these two companies, there are a few relatively small carriers of growing importance.

International air traffic

Deregulation of international air transport in Europe reached its final stage with the Third Air Liberalisation Package in 1993. Successive packages contained a wide variety of measures covering issues from licensing to air safety. However, their main thrust was the liberalisation of air traffic among EU countries. Any licensed EU carrier now has access to the routes between all airports in the EU regardless of destination or point of departure (but dependent on slot availability). Earlier, Member States regulated the sharing of capacity on each route and prices were fixed bilaterally.[95]

The major reason for the current financial troubles of Air France is that it was late in adjusting to fiercer competition. Losses soared to FF 6.7 billion, or 17 per cent of turnover, in 1993, indebtedness reached FF 35 billion and own capital was nearly wiped out. The sizeable losses are due to low productivity and high exploitation costs, as Air France is an expensive European carrier in terms of cost per passenger-kilometre (Curien et Jacobzone, 1993). For instance, the wage of a French pilot is about 20 per cent higher than that of an American pilot (Merlin, 1994). In addition, Air France appears to be overstaffed in the ticketing, sales and promotion sectors and the heterogeneity of its fleet leads to high maintenance costs. Many other European carriers suffer from the same problems, but some, such as British Airways and KLM, which have operated in a competitive environment for several years, have fared much better as their competitive edge has improved (Figure 20). International aviation liberalisation[96] is discussed in Box 4. International comparisons of the productivity of airline companies are fraught with methodological difficulties and estimated productivity differences vary widely in these studies (*Comité des Sages*, 1994, and Baily, 1993). They all

Figure 20. **AIRLINE PERFORMANCE**

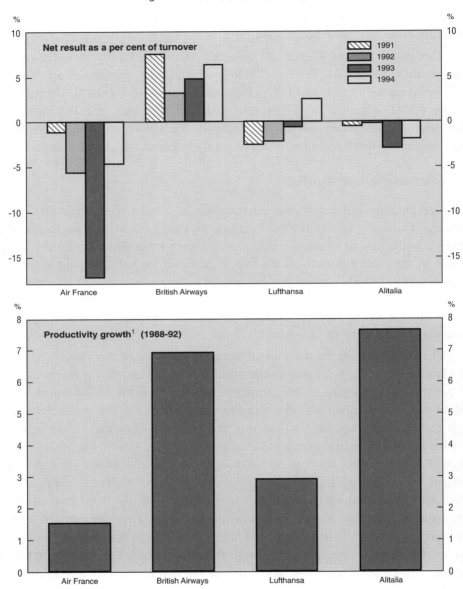

1. Available tonne-kilometres per employee.
Source: Comité des Sages (1994).

Box 4. Liberalisation of civil aviation markets

Deregulation enhances economic efficiency by curtailing unprofitable operations, promoting technological change and reducing the rents of organised groups. Airline deregulation in the late 1970s in the United States indeed led to lower air fares, a reorganisation of the market and the demise of unprofitable carriers (Winston, 1993). Consumers benefited greatly from a steep decline in air fares, and the annual economic benefits to travellers of lower air fares are estimated to range from $4.3 to $6.5 billion (at 1990 prices). In addition, flight frequency increased substantially. Deregulation was not at the expense of labour: relative wages changed little, while employment rose substantially. Liberalisation of the British and Dutch airline industries were similarly successful (Good *et al.*, 1993).

A significant feature of deregulation in the United States was the introduction of the "hub-and-spoke" system: passengers arriving on various incoming flights at one airport (the "hub") are quickly transferred and dispersed on outgoing flights. Previously, US carriers had to maintain numerous direct flights between various destinations with smaller planes. Passengers from relatively small communities have benefited from new connections through a hub, whereas business travellers have benefited from increased frequency. Operating a hub-and-spoke system does not necessarily improve the overall productivity performance, since costs increase due to additional airport handling. In Europe, only British Airways and KLM operate such a system.

Deregulation in the United States has not been without problems: the fast rise in traffic, and especially the operation of hub-and-spoke systems, have led to severe congestion problems as the Government failed to institute congestion pricing at major airports. In addition, "hubbing" may decrease competition, as carriers who have established a particular hub face little competition at their base. On the other hand, there has been no decline in air safety.

As charter carriers have a much larger market share in Europe and relatively short passenger flights increase inter-modal competition, gains from liberalisation are expected to be smaller than in the United States, and will most probably be found in cost reductions (Borenstein, 1992 and Good *et al.*, 1993). Air fares in Europe have not fallen markedly since 1989, when discount opportunities were implemented by the EC. This is in sharp contrast to the United States, where air fares fell immediately after the implementation of deregulation. Slow adjustment in Europe is likely to reflect the persisting lack of competition due to current slot allocation rules. On the other hand, fiercer competition on French domestic routes since early 1995 led to a dramatic fall in air fares on some connections.

conclude, however, that most European carriers suffer significantly from low productivity and that they are also high cost compared to American and Asian companies. Apart from cost and productivity problems, Air France did not follow other air carriers in pushing an international business strategy: because of its high prices it was not capable of establishing a hub and spoke system and it does not yet have many close international alliances, which would make it easier to exploit a much larger network.

In order to avoid bankruptcy, the State is providing massive financial support (FF 30 billion between 1992 and 1997) in exchange for ever more stringent restructuring plans (relations between the State and Air France are governed by a contract). In 1991, a first plan (*CAP* 93) entailed a capital injection of FF 5.8 billion[97] and a promise to reduce staff by 3 500. With losses rising further, a second plan (*plan de retour à l'équilibre*) provided for an additional transfer of FF 3 billion for 1993 and an additional cut in staff of 1 500. Another revised package, including more subsidies and further restructuring was rejected by the unions in October 1993. The latest plan (*Plan Blanc*) aims at an increase in productivity of 30 per cent over 3 years, a cut in the workforce of a further 5 000, a wage freeze until 1997 and a reduction in the fleet from 166 to 149 by 1999. As a counterpart, Air France will receive a ''last-time'' capital injection of FF 10 billion in 1994 and FF 5 billion in 1995 and 1996.[98] Due to the strong pickup in demand and the restructuring package, losses were more than halved in 1994 (FF 2.4 billion). On the other hand, fierce price competition continued and unit receipts fell again. The restructuring plan appears to be on schedule so far: the number of employees was reduced by 2 000, production costs fell by 7 per cent and investment plans were pruned. The current restructuring plan is likely to be the minimum required to improve the competitiveness of Air France, as it implies a return to profitability only in 1996. It is intended that the restructuring process lead to privatisation, but no deadline has been set.

The Commission (EC, 1994) considered that the latest capital injection constitutes a subsidy, as future profits are unlikely to yield a satisfactory return on the capital injection, and that it would distort competition among EU air carriers. However, the Commission still gave its go ahead, as it can provide a derogation for airline companies in financial trouble, if they draw up a viable restructuring plan, if financial difficulties are not transmitted to other companies and if the subsidisation process is transparent and controllable. Several airlines are seeking recourse against the Commission's ruling.

Domestic flights

Up until now, virtually all domestic flights (including those *outre-mer*) were accounted for by French carriers, reflecting the absence of cabotage rights. Air

Inter has realised a remarkable increase in traffic over the last decade, reaping the benefits of its dominant position in the domestic aviation market and the lack of competition. As a consequence, its financial performance has been much better than that of Air France in recent years. However, the latest recession and increased inter-modal competition, notably from the TGV, led to lower profits and finally a loss of FF 260 million in 1993. As with Air France, productivity is low and exploitation costs are high and, in addition, Air Inter has been required to cross-subsidise unprofitable routes. In view of fiercer competition in the future, cross-subsidisation has been ended and replaced by a new tax, levied on all passengers at French airports (FF 4 per ticket).

While Air Inter was in profit again in 1994, its immediate future does not appear to be rosy,[99] because cabotage will be fully phased in by 1 April 1997. This could lead to significant changes for Air Inter, as its domestic market will cease to be protected. Without restructuring, Air Inter projects losses of between FF 0.5 and 1 billion in the period 1995-97. Restructuring measures, which are so far much less radical than those for Air France, aim at a reduction in manning of 300 persons in 1995 and 1996, largely administrative staff. Work rules may also be revised and aligned more closely with the new Air France rules. As the European market will be completely open to competition by 1997, the Government plans to merge the European business of Air France with that of Air Inter. Air Inter will not only take over the European routes, but will also have to take 4 000 employees and 55 planes from Air France. A wave of strikes in the first months of 1995 have already cost an estimated FF 150 million and led to the shelving of the initial restructuring plan. A new one will be put forward.

Over the last two decades, smaller French regional and charter carriers have performed well owing to lower operating costs and better productivity, and their share in the French market (external and internal) rose from 5 per cent in 1975 to 21 per cent in 1993. However, they also suffered from the recession during 1993, when half of the more important regional and charter carriers sustained losses. Losses were highest at TAT (the British Airways controlled regional air carrier), as it aggressively tried to gain market shares, and as a percentage of turnover they were even higher than those of Air France.

Airport and slot management

There are 131 airports in France, of which two in the Paris area – Roissy-Charles de Gaulle (CDG) and Paris-Orly are the most important. All airports, except for those in Paris and Bale-Mulhouse, are publicly-owned, management being conceded to the Chambers of Commerce. Apart from CDG and Orly, which regularly show a profit and do not receive subsidies, all airports make losses or at best break even, and investment depends on state or local government subsidies. The Parisian airports are the second most important in Europe, after London, for passenger traffic and the third most important, after Frankfurt-am-Main and London, for freight traffic (Table 28). Owing to an ambitious investment programme over the last decade, they do not suffer from capacity problems, whereas some other European airports do, for instance London-Heathrow. Congestion problems at several large European airports are likely to impede competition, as current slot allocation mechanisms favour incumbent airlines. Despite the absence of congestion in France, new entrants had difficulties in obtaining international traffic rights to Orly and domestic traffic rights to Toulouse and Marseille. Since 1993 several air carriers have lodged complaints against the French authorities with the European Commission, which has decided in the carriers' favour.

Highly frequented airports have scheduling committees which allocate airport slots. The current rules favour established airlines and do not provide incentives for efficient allocation. Due to capacity constraints, airlines may not

Table 28. **Airports**

	Average annual growth 1980-90, in percentage	1990 level	Average annual growth 1990-93, in percentage	1993 level
1. Passengers (millions)				
Amsterdam	7.5	16.5	9.7	21.3
Frankfort	7.6	29.6	3.3	32.5
London	7.6	65.6	2.7	71.0
Paris	8.0	46.8	3.3	51.5
Rome	6.1	18.4	2.5	19.8
2. Air freight (million tonnes)				
Amsterdam	9.0	604.5	9.4	775
Frankfort	8.8	1 115.3	0.8	1 143
London	6.3	950.7	5.4	1 106
Paris	5.3	872.4	2.4	935
Rome	6.6	242.8	1.9	257

Source: INSEE.

get all the slots that they want and this often leads to (bilateral) barter trading between airlines. The EC's third liberalisation package has not changed the current allocation rules fundamentally, but it has ruled that all slots not used for 80 per cent of the time should be put into a pool for reallocation, 50 per cent of which should be available to new entrants. The arguments for road pricing can also be applied to airports – fees based on congestion and maintenance costs could reduce the need to increase airport capacity. Monetised trading of slots, rather than the present (bilateral) barter system, would set up a market in slots, similar to that operating at a few US airports. As the basic mission of airport management in France is to invest to an extent that avoids bottlenecks, such schemes are not envisaged here as they are in other countries. Introduction of such a system may also depend on co-operation at the EU-level.

Fluvial and maritime transport

Fluvial transport

The importance of fluvial transport has diminished sharply, with river-borne freight declining from 14 billion tonne-kilometres in 1970 to 6 billion tonne-kilometres in 1993, or only 3 per cent of the freight market. The persistent decline is predominantly caused by the fall in the transport of agricultural, food, petrol products and coal, whereas transport of construction material has remained stable. Since 1983, employment in this sector also has fallen markedly, from 6 100 to 2 700 in 1993. The Ministry of Transport issues shipping permits, while the *Voies navigables de France* (VNF), a joint state and shipper organisation, is responsible for the maintenance of the network, collection of taxes and distribution of subsidies.

France has an extensive network of canals and rivers, but only 2 000 km of it can be used by boats of more than 1 000 tonnes (Table 29). Approximately 700 out of the 2 800 French river boats are of this tonnage and it is only these larger boats that are cost competitive. Tarification is regulated: prices per kilometre decline with distance and are based on the average cost of transport by a self-propelled craft of 38.5 metres. This tarification system (established in 1964) is rather rigid and encourages transporters to use more flexible transport modes. Overcapacity and fixed prices have led to the *tour de rôle* (queuing) system of attributing freight loads. After the Commission ruled that the system was incom-

Table 29. **Inland waterways**

1992, in km

	France	Germany	United Kingdom	Italy	Netherlands
Length of network	8 533	4 350	2 353	1 366	5 046
of which: regularly used	5 881		1 192		
Length of network for capacity of craft exceeding 1 000 tonnes	2 004	3 120	794	1 108	2 398
of which: regularly used	1 844		662		

Source: UN.

patible with EC competition rules, it was reformed recently, but the new rules are far from liberal. As small craft are not competitive, this sector has been highly subsidised since 1986, mainly by *Electricité de France* (EDF), the energy monopoly. A water tax is levied on commercial users of water and, while most other users are exempted, EDF contributes FF 400 million a year to the VNF. In the context of the new regional policy plan, this will rise to almost FF 1 billion a year, which is likely to slow the pace of necessary reforms. Recently, the EDF formed an alliance with the *Companie nationale du Rhône* in order to build the missing links of the Rhine-Rhône canal by 2010. The estimated cost of FF 17.2 billion will be largely financed by the EDF. Project rate of return is projected to be very low, as receipts will not even cover the running costs of the canal.

Fluvial trade with foreign countries, Germany, Belgium and the Netherlands being the main partners, is in sizeable deficit (FF 364 million in 1993). In 1992, French craft only transported 23.3 per cent of all river trade between France and its neighbours. The French trade is predominantly concentrated on three axes: Rhine-Rhône, Seine-North and Seine-East. The most important river ports are Paris and Strasbourg with 25 and 10 billion tones of freight, respectively. French trade is particularly handicapped in comparison with Rotterdam and Antwerp, where river transport has a large share in the distribution of incoming goods. In 1987, about 50 per cent of all incoming goods in these two ports was distributed by water, whereas in Rouen this ratio was only 18 per cent.

Maritime transport

• Port services

French maritime ports have lost market shares, largely due to low rates of productivity growth (Table 30). In the past, the performance of French ports was crippled by rigid labour regulations and high strike activity. The dockers held large powers of decision over recruitment (layoffs were almost impossible) and the organisation of work-practices. In 1992, a reform of the dockers' statute was implemented. Employers regained their right to hire, and to impose more flexible work practices in general. In order to reduce overmanning, the reform was accompanied by social measures, the cost of which were particularly high[100] (FF 4 billion shared equally between the State and the ports). The reform, which will be phased-in by 1997, is expected to halve the number of dockers. However, the price competitiveness of French ports will remain crippled until then, due to the high social cost of the reform.

Large ports are managed by a state-appointed manager under the supervision of an administrative council consisting of representatives of the State, the local authority, port personnel, the chambers of commerce, complemented by experts.[101] The port authorities are responsible, *inter alia*, for infrastructural development, exploitation and maintenance of equipment, the police and development of industrial areas around the ports. They have to finance superstructural outlays (hangars, cranes, etc.). Exploitation costs are entirely financed by the

Table 30. **Throughput[1] in some European ports**

Average annual growth rates

	1970-80	1980-90	1991	1992	1993	Level[2] 1993
Rotterdam	2.4	0.4	1.5	0.5	−3.8	282.2
Antwerpen	−0.1	2.5	−0.7	2.3	−1.6	101.9
Marseille	3.4	−1.2	−2.4	1.2	−3.4	87.3
Hamburg	2.6	0.1	6.7	−0.6	1.1	65.8
London	−1.6	0.0	−8.3	−10.1	3.6	46.1
Le Havre	2.9	−3.5	5.9	−7.2	3.6	55.0
Dunkerque	4.9	−1.2	11.5	−1.2	1.5	40.8

1. Goods loaded and unloaded.
2. Million tonnes.
Source: ECMT and Gemeentelijk Havenbedrif Rotterdam.

independent ports by means of port related taxes (for instance, levies on incoming ships), rental of facilities and property taxes. The State pays for all charges related to exploitation of locks, channels, the outer-harbour and protective sea-dykes. It also contributes 80 per cent of all costs related to the deepening of waterways and the extension of channels, as well as 60 per cent of other infra-structural outlays, *e.g.* dry-dock equipment. In short, the State subsidises ports significantly. This has, however, not been sufficient to improve the competitive position of French ports. More independence, a stronger business orientation and a strong boost in productivity will be needed in order to regain market shares. The port of Rotterdam, for example, is managed independently, and a strong commercial strategy has developed, along with high rates of productivity growth.

- The fleet

About 80 French companies exploit 216 French ships (with another 105 'French' ships registered in other countries), although the fleet is predominantly concentrated among four firms (Table 31). The fleet has been in decline for decades, is old (14 years on average in 1993) and is rather small (sixth in tonnage among the 15 EU Member countries). Between 1980 and 1990 alone its global market share, in terms of tonnage shipped, diminished from 3 to 1 per cent. Several factors have contributed to this decline: *i)* the loss of the colonial empire, *ii)* high wage and non-wage costs, and *iii)* increasing competition from low-cost countries, international shipping being largely open to competition. Recently, the European Commission has started to act in the field of competition, investigating the role of conferences in restricting competition. Several shipping companies, including French ones, have been fined for sharing out traffic between European and African countries.

Table 31. **The fleet**

1992

	France	Germany	United Kingdom	Italy	Netherlands
Number of ships	216	869	425	928	416
Tonnage (thousands)	3 215	4 975	3 367	7 087	2 801

Source: ECSA, 1993.

Competition should also heat up in the future with the introduction of EU-wide cabotage for vessels registered in an EU Member country. Rules concerning staffing and other conditions are still disparate, depending on the size of the vessel, whether services are mainland or island oriented, etc. Mediterranean countries, including France, have temporary exemptions from implementing cabotage regulation along the Mediterranean and Atlantic coasts: these cover transport of strategic goods (until 1 January 1997), services by small units (until 1 January 1998), and regular ferry services (until 1 January 1999). Services to French islands in the Mediterranean and overseas departments are also excluded until 1 January 1999.

V. Conclusions

In the 1993-1994 Survey of France, both the depth of the 1993 recession and the speed of the recovery were underestimated. Indeed, growth accelerated significantly during 1994 to reach close to 4 per cent by the end of the year. On a yearly average, GDP growth of 2³/₄ per cent was in line with the European Union average. The upswing first benefited from strong foreign demand and a halt in the run-down of inventories. Since mid-1994 final domestic demand components have also shown considerable strength. Employment reacted faster and more positively to the recovery than during earlier upswings, and grew more quickly than in the other large European countries. The unemployment rate fell by ³/₄ percentage point. This performance could be a sign that labour market reforms undertaken since the late 1980s are now showing results. The persistence of labour market slack has led to very low wage increases, and consumer price inflation has remained stable, at about 1³/₄ per cent, over the last year. The prices of manufactured goods have risen somewhat faster recently, but disinflation in the service sector has continued. Despite the swift rise in import volumes, the trade and current account balances have remained in surplus.

GDP could expand at a steady rate of around 3 per cent until the end of 1996, the 1995 Budget amendments and associated measures having little effect on growth. This will allow a gradual decline in cyclical slack and a fall in the unemployment rate, while employment growth is projected to remain fairly robust. Growth will be driven by strong business investment, reflecting substantial profits, healthy balance sheets and a favourable domestic and foreign demand outlook. A fast rise in investment will boost the growth of potential, an important condition for perpetuating strong growth at low rates of inflation later in the upswing. Private consumption should also strengthen, due to employment growth and a further fall in the saving ratio. Export growth is likely to remain strong, even though the recovery in imports implies a negative foreign sector contribution to growth. As a result of the VAT rate increase, inflation could accelerate to 2½ per cent in the first half of 1996, before dropping back in the second half of the year, as lower indirect labour costs reduce cost pressures and partially offset the effects of the VAT increase. Inflation could be higher if margins do not react symmetrically to the VAT increase and labour cost reductions. Although the recovery has become well established, it cannot be excluded that the strength of investment is overestimated. Apart from somewhat weaker foreign and domestic demand growth – evident in recent business surveys – the effects of the recent sharp exchange rate changes on foreign demand remain uncertain. In addition, short-term interest rates may not fall from their current high level as fast as assumed in the projections. If a strong pickup in investment does not materialise, bottlenecks could appear earlier than expected, as weak capital formation since the early 1990s has lowered the growth of potential. A swift reduction in the government deficit, which would leave more room for rapid growth in the private sector, would reduce such a risk.

An encouraging feature of this recovery has been its strong employment content. Wage moderation in the private sector was probably crucial in achieving a better employment performance, although it is difficult to disentangle the effects of active labour market measures, such as the significant rise in public sector employment programmes, the implementation of measures to raise labour market flexibility, and low wage growth. But the example of other OECD countries demonstrates that modest rises in labour costs lead to a favourable employment performance, and in 1994 the wage bill rose more as a result of employment gains than wage rate increases.

These favourable developments are partly due to the change in the orientation of labour-market policies since the late 1980s. Then, the emphasis was on early retirement programmes, which reduced labour force participation. This was very costly and such programmes have been scaled down. In addition, many active labour market programmes were selective, with shifting emphases on long-term and youth unemployment. They usually had the desired effect on the targeted group, but strong substitution effects meant that few jobs were created overall. Over recent years, the emphasis of labour market policy has moved away from treating the social impact of unemployment towards providing employment programmes and raising incentives to look for work. For example, in 1992, the social partners agreed to unemployment benefits being paid on a downward sliding scale over time and a small cut in the total benefit period. The multi-year labour market programme, which was implemented during 1994, continues and extends earlier government efforts to reduce structural unemployment. It places emphasis on raising labour market flexibility and lowering labour costs for the least qualified, who suffer the highest rates of unemployment. The programme provides incentives to move away from rigid working hours, the specifics being negotiated by the social partners. However, this option has been exercised only infrequently so far, and more may have to be done to increase flexibility. The programme also contains measures to reduce social security contributions for low skilled workers, in order to raise labour demand in the private services sector. In addition, it aims at the decentralisation of existing training programmes and a further move towards on-the-job training. The programme also streamlined the number of labour market programmes, but many still remain and a greater effort should be made to evaluate their effectiveness.

After rising steadily for many years, the rate of structural unemployment may have stabilised at around 9 per cent since the late 1980s, although it is especially difficult to estimate precisely. It is, however, likely to be among the highest in the OECD. This poses serious social problems and is why a substantial reduction in unemployment is a top priority of the new Government. The Government's strategy is two-fold: a reduction in indirect labour costs for the least qualified, and the pursuit of specific measures for the long-term unemployed. Programmes that reduce indirect labour costs will be stepped up – a move in the right direction. Stronger incentives will be provided for hiring long-term unemployed people, who risk losing human capital, face serious social problems and could forfeit any prospect of finding a job. The details of another, more generous, youth training programme are currently being negotiated with the social partners. However, these measures are again selective and could have substitution and windfall effects. In order to avoid such effects, it would probably have been better to have gone further in reducing indirect labour costs on hiring low-skilled workers than is proposed in the Budget amendments. But large cuts in indirect labour costs inevitably pose a difficult financing problem. The rise in corporate taxes will raise business costs, although this will be offset by other measures, and the higher VAT rate will feed into both price increases and higher wages. In summary, financing through higher taxation risks diluting the potential positive employment effects of lower labour costs. Cutting lower priority government expenditure would have been preferable. The logic of seeking to lower non-wage labour costs for the least skilled is in large part to remedy the negative effects of high and rigid minimum wages on the employment prospects of new job seekers with low skill levels. From this perspective, it would seem more coherent to seek over time to lower minimum wages relative to average wages, rather than to raise them further as the new Government has decided to do. While there is a continuing debate internationally about the employment effects of minimum wages, with some studies suggesting that those effects are quite small, the evidence is largely drawn from countries where the ratio of the minimum to the median wage is substantially smaller than in France. Relatively high minimum wages have been defended on equity grounds, but to the extent that they lead to unemployment, there is doubt about their effectiveness in this regard. Greater flexibility in the minimum wage system might necessitate changes to the current system of income support. It could, for instance, be provided by some form of earned income tax credit. This would raise work incentives and keep the social safety net intact.

Substantial savings would need to be generated elsewhere in the public sector in order to finance a more ambitious job creation scheme. According to OECD estimates, the structural deficit has risen since 1987; in particular the upward phase of the previous cycle was not used to lower the deficit sufficiently and little progress was made in reducing it in 1994. Despite stronger than expected growth and a considerable reform effort in the social security area, overall net lending remained at 6 per cent of GDP and the government debt, on a Maastricht definition, reached 48.5 per cent of GDP (compared with 35.4 per cent in 1990). Moreover, the State used the revenue windfall resulting from stronger growth to finance additional expenditure. Although the deficit target was respected, the objective of freezing outlays in real terms – announced in the initial Budget and confirmed in the medium-term fiscal programme voted in early 1994 – was not attained. While improving, the social security deficit fell by less than expected, in spite of the fact that reforms of the health, pension and unemployment insurance systems led to a significant deceleration in spending. This was because social security revenues were much lower than expected, partly due to exemptions from social security contributions for certain segments of the labour market, which are not all compensated by the State.

The original 1995 Budget implied considerable expenditure restraint. However, significant overspending and revenue shortfalls were recorded in the first half of 1995. The Budget amendments, presented in late June 1995, include new employment programmes and a general cut in employers' social security contributions for low-income earners. New spending initiatives and fiscal slippage in the first half of 1995 will be covered by direct and indirect tax increases (close to 1 per cent of GDP on a full year basis) in order to maintain the initial 1995 deficit level for the State. According to the official projections, general government net borrowing will fall to 5 per cent of GDP in 1995 and 4 per cent in 1996. However, additional measures will be needed if the 1996 objective is to be met. The deficit cut looks meagre on an international comparison – many other OECD countries have taken much firmer action to reduce their deficits. According to the OECD's medium-term scenario, which assumes no further policy initiatives, an additional effort will be needed in order to achieve the official objective of a deficit of 3 per cent of GDP in 1997.

A tax increase may be justified in order to reduce the deficit quickly and rein in debt accumulation, but given the high and rising level of taxation, efforts should concentrate on the expenditure side: the number of public officials is high on an international comparison, suggesting room for streamlining operations and reducing overlap among ministries. More emphasis on evaluating the costs and benefits of government programmes should help in guiding action to reduce outlays. Given the large weight of wages in total expenditure, only modest pay rises for public officials will be a necessary condition for fulfilling the government's expenditure target of no spending growth in real terms. Public sector salary increases have easily outstripped those in the private sector in recent years. Moreover, means-testing of transfer payments could be extended. In the social security area, health care reforms need to be continued, especially in the hospital sector, and the special pension schemes should be reformed. Finally, the reform of public enterprises, which receive a considerable amount of state aid, should be accelerated.

Rapid cuts in deficits would help in smoothing the impact of demographic changes on government finances, which could be considerable in the long run. The 1993 reform of the general pension system was a first major step in the right direction, and further increases in contribution rates are scheduled for the complementary schemes over the coming years. These measures are likely to keep the general scheme broadly in balance until 2010. In addition to the general pension scheme, special schemes exist, *inter alia* for government employees and those in some state-owned enterprises, and these have not yet been reformed. Given the generosity of some of the schemes, a rapid rise in spending is likely, entailing a rise in contribution rates, higher government funding, or increases in taxation. In addition, the impact of ageing on public finances is likely to be felt strongly again after 2010. Simulations by the OECD suggest that, after that time, population ageing could lead to a rapid rise in the pension system's and overall deficits, which could double the debt/GDP ratio. As the pension age in France is considerably lower than in many other OECD countries, and as life expectancy is probably increasing further, raising the pension age would appear to be a relatively attractive means of avoiding such a deficit increase. Mandatory action seems preferable, as increasing the contributory period necessary to obtain a full pension, as in the 1993 pension reform, may not raise the effective pension age sufficiently. If the retirement age is not lifted, contribution rates will need to be further augmented, or the generosity of the system considerably pruned. Another option would be to aim at a sizeable primary surplus at the general government level by the turn of the century, which would lead to much more favourable debt dynamics.

The goal of monetary policy is internal and external currency stability. The central bank's objectives are inflation of less than 2 per cent, medium-term growth of the money supply of no more than 5 per cent, and a stable exchange rate *vis-à-vis* the core ERM countries. The Government attaches great importance to the stability of the exchange rate in the context of the realisation of European Monetary Union. The Maastricht criteria for inflation and long-term interest rates are currently being met and this performance is likely to continue until 1996. Despite the excellent inflation performance, the franc has come under pressure on several occasions since 1992, the markets judging the policy mix to be unbalanced. While fiscal policy cushioned the cyclical downturn between 1990 and 1993, monetary policy was kept tight in order to keep the franc close to its central parity in the ERM. Exchange market pressures since September 1992 have been fended off four times by temporarily raising short-term interest rates sharply. Between mid-1992 and mid-1995, with the exception of 1994, France was the only G7 country where the yield curve was flat or inverted. In addition, M3 has been growing below its limit since 1993. The recurrent episodes of currency turbulence in the ERM show the necessity of improving overall economic performance through macroeconomic policies and structural reforms

While tight monetary policies since the early 1990s have led to lower nominal long-term interest rates, they have remained higher than in the other hard-core ERM countries between mid-1992 and mid-1995. The persistence of differentials against Germany probably reflects a long memory of France's inflationary history up until the mid-1980s and, more recently, preoccupations with public finances. With inflation remaining under control, further gains in credibility could be achieved over the coming years. However, credibility needs to be underpinned by solid economic fundamentals. In this respect, financial markets attach great importance to sound fiscal policies, and a significant cut in the government deficit should reduce uncertainties in financial markets and lower risk premia.

Lower short-term interest rates would improve the situation in the banking sector. Several banks and insurance companies have slid into financial problems since 1993. Loan loss provisions have risen sharply and a couple of banks and insurance companies have had to hive off doubtful assets into a separate company in order to comply with prudential supervision rules. The State has also provided support to five banks and one insurance company. The most important case is the rescue package for *Crédit Lyonnais*. Officially estimated potential losses amount to FF 50 billion – an estimate surrounded by large uncertainties. They should be largely covered by the capital gains from selling profitable assets and the retention of a large share of future profits, which will be boosted by a restructuring plan. While the short-term budgetary burden is likely to be low, future costs are difficult to assess. In addition to the eventual implications for public finances, the *Crédit Lyonnais* case has raised questions as to whether internal and external controls should be strengthened and, more generally, corporate governance issues. It would seem important that the responsibility for prudential supervision and assessing implications for competition be clearly separated from shareholder interests. Eventually, it would seem desirable to privatise *Crédit Lyonnais*.

Both overall growth and the effectiveness of macroeconomic policies could be enhanced by reforms of goods and services markets. The transport sector, examined in depth in this Survey, is a good example in this respect. France has an extensive transport network, which is in very good shape in physical terms.

However, changes in transport policies could lead to efficiency gains and, at the same time, reduce public spending. The sector was heavily regulated until the mid-1980s. Intervention by the State has been scaled back since then, but it remains important in setting the rules for competition and in shaping overall developments, either directly or *via* state-owned enterprises, with EU-wide policies and local government playing an increasing role. Relations between the State, local authorities and state-owned enterprises are guided by contracts, and market mechanisms play only a minor role. However, auctions have been introduced in the airline industry, a mechanism which could be used more extensively.

The government, local authorities and state-owned enterprises provide most of the transport infrastructure, but – as in most other OECD countries – the majority of users do not pay the full cost of its use. For example, despite the existence of a motorway toll system since 1955, it has only recently been used for traffic management purposes, and rents on profitable motorway sections are increasingly used to build unprofitable ones. Recent experiments on a limited scale show that changes in tolls can have a considerable impact on traffic flows. While all large projects are subject to a financial evaluation, regional policy considerations weigh heavily in final investment decisions, and many of the future TGV and motorway projects will not be profitable. Judging from past experience – and in line with policies in many other countries – it seems easier for the public authorities to raise the supply of infrastructure than to change taxes and prices. Prices are also distorted because environmental, safety and congestion costs are seldom taken fully into account. The charges for road haulage, for instance, are far below social costs.

Even if unpopular, it would appear important to move closer to a more rational pricing system. This would lead to a better use of existing facilities, thereby increasing the transport sector's rate of return and growth contribution and remedying distortions in inter-modal competition. Finally, it would give planners clear signals of future demand, current planning being based on distorted prices. Charging for all social costs would mean that users would face the full cost of transport services, and move towards the (quality-adjusted) least-cost mode. Efficiency considerations may be overruled by public service obligations, which play an important role in the French context, accessibility to transport services at a "fair" price is enshrined in transport law. These aims can be achieved by either providing transfers to individuals or by subsidising transport enterprises. Subsidisation is likely to be a second-best solution in most cases and subsidies should be provided in a transparent way.

Liberalisation of the transport sector has increased intra-modal and inter-modal competition and raised the pace of required structural adjustment significantly. The road freight sector, where liberalisation has gone furthest, has probably adjusted best, while the SNCF, which is not yet subject to intra-modal competition, has had difficulties in accelerating the pace of restructuring. The pace of change has been slower in the public airlines than has been the case in other countries, despite growing competition pressure arising from EU policies, and almost non-existent in the Parisian urban transport system. While lower transport prices since liberalisation in some areas have benefited consumers, as taxpayers they face a heavy bill for financing state assistance to public transport enterprises (an estimated FF 50 billion in 1994). The financial problems of the SNCF are caused by stiff competition from the road transport sector, little commercial freedom, and very rigid work practices. Reforms appear urgent, as the situation is likely to deteriorate further, which could lead to a dramatic rise in debt levels. So far, only one of the SNCF's problems has been tackled: responsibility for regional passenger services is being passed to the regions, which should raise incentives to streamline loss-making services. A freeing up of railway services, which might happen on an EU-wide scale, could make much deeper reforms necessary. In moving towards the separation of the network and services provision, France could usefully learn from German and Swedish experience in this domain. Restructuring of public airlines is also difficult and costly. Slow adjustment to fierce competition is the major reason for the current financial problems of Air France. In order to avoid bankruptcy, the State is providing massive financial support for ever more stringent restructuring packages. The latest plan aims at an increase in productivity of 30 per cent over 3 years. It seems to be the minimum required to ensure the viability of the enterprise. Restructuring of Air Inter, the other nationalised airline, which is now facing more competition on domestic routes than earlier, has started slowly.

Transport-related expenditure and revenue flows between the public and private sector are considerable and changes in policies could help in attaining the government's medium-term fiscal commitments. Action to lower expenditure could involve more efficient use of existing infrastructure by bringing prices closer to scarcity values, thus reducing the need to invest in infrastructure. Future investment would also be lower if the ambitious regional policy component were scaled back to those projects for which the beneficial regional growth effects can be demonstrated clearly. Finally, and most importantly, the structural adjustment of lagging sectors needs to be accelerated, otherwise large subsidies, as well as the need to assume large amounts of debt, could burden future tax payers. On the other hand, reducing current distortions, for instance by raising the diesel tax, could be an important source of additional tax revenue. In addition, road tolls on heavily travelled motorway sectors could be raised, although it would be important that the resulting revenues be used in the most effective way, and not necessarily ploughed back into further motorway development.

Structural reforms of product markets have progressed in other areas. The privatisation programme has continued, and since 1993 eight enterprises have been fully or partially privatised, yielding FF 114 billion. This programme should lead to efficiency gains and contribute to an improvement in the public accounts, which are still burdened with payments for recapitalisation and state aids to ailing public enterprises. In the first half of 1995, there were only two asset sales, but the new Government has decided to accelerate the pace of privatisation. In 1994, a programme to support the creation and development of small and medium-sized enterprises was passed by parliament. It includes: tax cuts, equal legal treatment with corporations, improved social protection for the self-employed, and a streamlining of administrative procedures, although this has not yet been implemented. Health reform continued in 1994 with the implementation of medical guidelines for doctors, and payments for treatment and prescriptions rose considerably less than in 1993. On the other hand, little progress has been made in the reform of the hospital sector. Moreover, liberalisation of the energy market has not yet begun, and the deregulation of certain telecommunications services could progress faster. The large state-owned enterprises in the energy and telecommunication sectors are not yet on the privatisation list. While Sunday shop-opening hours have become more liberal, licensing of large retail outlets remains restrictive.

In summary, a robust recovery became firmly established during 1994 and, in contrast to some other OECD countries, inflation should not pose a threat to the sustainability of strong future growth, despite the price level increase induced by the rise in the VAT rate. An encouraging aspect of the recovery is the fairly rapid growth in the number of employees – 1¾ per cent in the year to

March 1995 – which reflects not only significant wage moderation, but also the impact of labour market reforms over recent years. Current circumstances are particularly favourable for accelerating the pace of structural adjustment. In this respect high priority should be given to public sector reforms, in order to rapidly reduce the sizeable government deficit. The objective of cutting the deficit to 3 per cent of GDP in 1997 appears to be a minimum, as the economy could then be close to the peak of the cycle. As the new Government has set an ambitious job creation objective, controlling expenditure has become even more important. New measures should be financed by cuts in low priority spending areas. An increase in taxation is a second best solution, as it mainly redistributes income, with only a limited impact on net job creation at best. Fiscal consolidation based on expenditure restraint is unlikely to dent growth significantly – as demonstrated by experience in other countries. On the contrary, it should inspire confidence in financial markets, contribute to lowering interest rates, and free resources for strong and non-inflationary private sector growth.

Notes

1. Employment in the service sector includes people who, although employed by temporary employment agencies, often work outside the service sector.

2. Changes in overtime, bonuses and short-time work had much less effect on the differences between hourly and per-capita pay in 1993 and 1994.

3. This measure of underlying inflation excludes food, energy and tobacco, as well as fiscal measures.

4. The higher rates of the consumer price index are largely due to the above-average rise in the rent component of the consumer price index and indirect tax increases.

5. The failure to explain recent price developments is not due to a lack of understanding of wage developments.

6. It cannot be ruled out that the tracking is poor outside the estimation period, because such low rates of inflation as in 1994 have not been observed inside it. Price adjustment, for instance, could become slower at very low rates of inflation.

7. The official sector includes the *Trésor public*, the *Banque de France*, *La Poste*, the *Caisse française de développement*, the *Crédit national* for lending and grants by the French Government to foreign governments, and local authorities.

8. Certain African countries which were French colonies before independence and which have their exchange rates linked with the French franc.

9. The Maastricht Treaty also stipulates that the normal European Exchange Rate (ERM) fluctuation bands must be respected without severe tensions in the two years prior to the (1996) assessment of whether the Maastricht criteria are being met. However, there is, so far, no official definition of what constitutes severe tension.

10. The same result is found in a recent IMF study (Ostry and Levy, 1994).

11. The specification of the money demand function is the same as the one presented in the 1994 Annual Survey of Germany (see Annex I of that Survey for a more detailed description). The money demand function is based on an error correction model, where first a long-run level relationship between real money $(m - p)$, output (y) and short (IRS) and long-run (IRL) interest rates is estimated. m, y and p are expressed in natural logs, t indicates the period, t-statistics are in parenthesis and the estimation period is from 1978 to 1994, estimation being on half-yearly data:

$$EC(t-1) = 0.99 \ y(t-1) + 1.83 \ IRS(t-1) - 2.63 \ IRL(t-1) - (m-p)(t-1)$$
$$\quad\quad (1416.3) \quad\quad (4.5) \quad\quad\quad (-7.0)$$

In a second stage a dynamic relationship is estimated in first differences, including the error correction term (EC) in levels. Δ is the change operator:

$$\Delta m(t) = 0.01 + 0.43 \ \Delta m(t-1) + 0.33 \ \Delta y(t-1) + 0.42 \ \Delta p(t-1) + 0.33 \ \Delta IRS(t-1) - 0.23 \ EC(t-1)$$
$$\quad\quad (1.0) \quad (2.7) \quad\quad\quad (1.0) \quad\quad\quad (2.3) \quad\quad\quad (0.9) \quad\quad\quad (-2.0)$$

$$\text{Adj.} R^2 = 0.53 \quad\quad S.E.E = 0.016 \quad\quad D.W. = 2.1$$

The results of the equation are standard and close to that for Germany, except for the positive effect of short-term interest rates. The latter is likely to reflect the importance of money market funds in France in the M3 measure, money market fund placements reacting strongly to changes in the yield curve.

12. In the case of the insurance company, large losses arose in a real estate credit subsidiary and State aid was provided in the form of a transfer of shares from two other state-owned enterprises.

13. It consisted of a capital injection of FF 4.9 billion (of which FF 3.5 billion came from the State), a State contribution of FF 4 billion to the special corporate vehicle in 1994 and 1995 and a State guarantee of FF 12.4 billion for doubtful assets put into a special structure.

14. Eight members are nominated by the State and two members by the bank.

15. The budget projected a rise in consumer prices of 2.2 per cent in 1994. The outcome was 1.7 per cent.

16. Additional detail on the 1994 Budget is contained in the previous Survey.

17. Revenues earmarked for capital injections are booked in a special account and do not affect data in Table 11.

18. The initial 1995 Budget projected that FF 47 billion, out of a total of FF 55 billion, in privatisation receipts would be used to finance current expenditure. The initial 1995 deficit, on a Maastricht basis, was, therefore, equivalent to FF 322 billion as compared to FF 275 billion on the former accounting basis. In the amended 1995 Budget, privatisation receipts – the projected amount of which was revised down from FF 55 billion to FF 40 billion – will only be used for capital injections for public enterprises (FF 14.5 billion) and debt reduction (FF 24.5 billion).

19. This tax is used to partly compensate the adverse effects of demographic differences between the pension insurance schemes.

20. In Germany consolidation started even during the recession, the structural improvement between 1991 and 1996 being estimated at 4 percentage points.

21. Caution needs to be exercised in interpreting these numbers. For example, the split between public and private activity in areas such as health and education, differs considerably across countries.

22. The health and pension systems were the theme of the special chapter in the previous Survey.

23. The spending generated by their activities is the subject to targets set annually, after negotiation with the health professionals, which are accompanied by penalties in the event of overruns (except in the case of pharmaceuticals).

24. Measures included indexation of pensions to prices, a gradual increase in the length of contributions over a 10-year period starting in 1994 and the calculation of pensions on the basis of the wage earned during the best 25 rather than the best 10 years. These measures will all be in force by 1 January 2008, the transition taking 15 years.

25. Since 1994, the *FSV* has been financed by part of the *Contribution sociale généralisée (CSG)* revenues (1.3 percentage points) and excise taxes on beverages.

26. The assumptions are that consumer prices will increase by 2 per cent per year and the average wage by 3 per cent per year.

27. According to the *Livre blanc sur les retraites* (1991), the number of people contributing to the civil servants' scheme in 2010 will be 1.9 million (as in 1990), while the number of recipients will be 1.3 million, compared to 0.8 million in 1990. Assuming little change in the demographic compensation mechanism, 45 per cent of benefits would remain unfunded in 2010 unless there is a reform.

28. In addition, the health spending/GDP ratio could rise by 2 percentage points between 2000 and 2030 due to the ageing of the population, while large offsets on education spending are unlikely.

29. In France the pension age is currently 60 years. By around 2010 no other large OECD country will have a retirement age below 65 years. Increases in the pension age are all phased in over many years.

30. The scheduled rise in contribution rates of the complementary schemes is already taken into account in the baseline scenario.

31. The difference between physical and financial assets and liabilities.

32. If the national reference area is exceeded, the new CAP provides for penalties in the form of additional land to be set aside for which there is no compensation, and reduced subsidies. With France having exceeded its reference area by 1.3 per cent in 1994, the following rate is set to increase by 1.3 per cent in 1995, while income support for producers will decline commensurately.

33. According to the financial report by the European Agricultural Guidance and Guarantee Fund (EAGGF), 23½ per cent of EAGGF spending in 1993 went to France, compared with some 14 per cent to Germany and Italy and 8 per cent to the United Kingdom.

34. With government stocks of cereals having risen by two-thirds over the period 1991-93, subsidies for cereal storage increased sharply, from FF 1.8 to 8.6 billion. Such expenditure should fall as a result of the reform of the CAP, but did not do so in 1993.

35. These are programmes reducing taxation, measures to help young farmers start up, aid programmes for farm modernisation involving capital grants and interest rate subsidies, compensation for natural disasters and marketing aid. Also, the EU, in conjunction with member States, co-finances other policies with various objectives such as promoting diversification, early retirement for farmers, improving infrastructure, schemes to encourage R&D and measures in favour of rural development.

36. The rate of contribution to the farmers' pension scheme is 8.7 per cent, *i.e.* 13 percentage points less than the average (*Livre blanc sur les retraits*, 1991).

37. The effective fall in cereal prices brought them more into line with world prices, which had strengthened as a result of the dollar's weakness, flooding in the United States and the drought in Australia. When world supplies return to normal, however, the decline in prices will improve the competitiveness of non-Community cereals.

38. Pharmaceuticals, construction equipment, medical equipment, iron and steel, beer, furniture, farm equipment and spirits.

39. The agreement on intellectual property provides for the application of the general principles of the GATT (national treatment and non-discrimination) and defines the rules aimed at protecting royalties, patents, brands, designs and models, integrated circuits and marks of the country of origin.

40. This mainly involves temporary exemption from business tax for the creation and expansion of firms (5 years) and also from social security contributions (1 year).

41. These two funds' resources come, on the one hand, from a tax of FF 4 per passenger paid by the airline companies and, on the other, from taxes on hydroelectric works and motorway tolls.

42. Supermarket floor space increased by 1.7 million m^2 in 1991, 1.9 million m^2 in 1992 and 0.2 million m^2 in 1993.

43. The long-term unemployed represent 57 per cent of the total number of registered unemployed in Belgium and 47 per cent in the Netherlands.

44. Expenditure on employment was financed in the following proportions: 20 per cent by employers and occupational schemes, 43 per cent by the unemployment insurance scheme, and 37 per cent by central and local government.

45. In a number of schemes, the government does not bear the cost of the exemptions from employers' contributions, so that the receipts of the social security schemes are reduced accordingly. This effect is not shown in the table.

46. The SMIC is raised annually in line with consumer prices, and must increase by at least 50 per cent of the increase in the real overall average wage. Wage equations (official estimates) suggest that real SMIC increases are passed on to the overall wage with a relatively low long-term elasticity (0.087, a figure slightly higher than the proportion of wage-earners being paid the SMIC – 8.2 per cent). The effect is much greater, however, on the wages of young people: a 10 per cent increase in the minimum wage leads in the long term to an increase of about 7 per cent in the youth wage (OECD, 1995b, and Bazen and Martin, 1991).

47. The top rate for employers' family allowance contributions corresponds to 5.4 per cent of the gross wage.

48. The switch to part-time work must be followed by the hiring of a part-time worker on an indefinite-term contract so as to keep the same number of hours worked in the firm.

49. The number of hours can vary between 16 and 32 a week, compared with 19 to 30 previously, and can be calculated on an annual basis (see below).

50. Employees on short-time work receive an allowance at least equal to half of their net reference wage for hours worked in excess of the 700 hours of the current quota for short-time work, up to a maximum of 1 200 hours over 18 months.

51. On the other hand, the relatively long duration of benefits has only a slight impact on long-term unemployment among under-25 and over-50 year-olds. The young unemployed often do not meet the requirements regarding the minimum period of affiliation to the unemployment insurance scheme, while older workers can qualify for early retirement benefits.

52. As from 1993, the unemployment insurance scheme distributes a single degressive benefit which replaces the former basic and end-of-entitlement benefits, and also the exceptional benefit. The benefit payment period ranges from 4 to 60 months, depending on the length of affiliation and age. Thus, the unemployed aged 55 and over draw benefit at the normal rate for 27 months, and then at a rate which diminishes by 8 per cent every 4 months for 33 months, so that they receive an income until they reach the legal retirement age.

53. These two measures are of a six months' duration. They are funded by the employer laying off staff, the social partners and the State, while beneficiaries receive 80 per cent of their last wage.

54. In fact, the situation is even more complicated because many other bodies are involved in employment policy. The AFPA and numerous regional bodies are responsible for occupational training, the APEC (*Association pour l'emploi des cadres*) finds jobs for managerial grades, the *Délégation à l'emploi* and the *Fonds national de l'emploi* administer a number of active measures, etc. This explains why, in a study on how the implementation of employment policy is organised in the EU (Höcker, 1994), France is ranked among the "countries with a fragmented system".

55. The OEST (*Observatoire Economique et Statistique des Transports*), a joint INSEE and Transport Ministry institute, provides an extensive annual review of transport sector developments in the *Comptes des Transports de la Nation*.

56. This figure refers to the transport service sector in a National Accounts perspective.

57. Two-thirds of the current network (excluding TGV lines) are used by only 20 per cent of the passengers and are unprofitable.

58. Even on the North-South axis traffic density is only half that of the most heavily used motorways in other parts of Europe.

59. Some characteristics of the transport sector seem to change little, even over centuries. Harmelle summarises the impressions of Arthur Young's trip through France in 1789 as follows: "*Parcourant la route royale de Paris à Toulouse, il s'émerveille de l'état des routes françaises. Elles sont les plus belles d'Europe, dit-il, les mieux construites, les mieux entretenues, les plus larges. Mais il les trouve désespérément vides de trafic, alors que les chemins boueux et malcommodes de l'Angleterre de la même époque sont encombrés de charrois*" (quoted after Offner, 1993).

60. She uses two infrastructure capital series, one including and one excluding roads. The broader definition, including roads, leads to lower elasticity estimates.

61. The Act on Inland Transport states that transport policy should aim at sustainable mobility and accessibility at a "fair" price.

62. The common transport policy did not include air and maritime traffic, even though other policies, such as competition, internal market and commercial policies should have applied to them.

63. Recent publications by the *Commissariat Général du Plan* (1992 and 1993) and the *Rapport Boiteux* (1994) provide a good overview of the current discussion on transport policy in France.

64. Railways were nationalised because of their poor financial position and not for natural monopoly considerations.

65. Currently project evaluation is based on different macroeconomic assumptions, different values for time or life saved and different parameters in evaluating environmental effects. In addition, it does not always take account of inter-modal consequences of projects.

66. Contrary to most other transport sectors, its operating environment has not changed, and it faces little competition and deficits are covered *ex post*.

67. The *train à grande vitesse* (TGV) is France's high speed train.

68. Huart (1994) summarises several studies which are all very limited in scope. He concludes that TGV projects had only small, local effects on business and employment creation.

69. Extensive toll road systems also exist in Italy, Japan and the United States.

70. Concessions are granted for very long periods, thus, there is no auctioning of concessions at set intervals.

71. From the start, concession holders were financially supported by the State and their debt state-guaranteed through the *Caisse nationale des autoroutes*.

72. Recent EC directives have allowed for two different infrastructure charging policies, tolls on the basis of the distance travelled, and user charges on the basis of the time the road network is used. Germany, the Netherlands, Denmark, Belgium and Luxembourg introduced a common user charge system at the beginning of 1995. Although this system is less costly to implement – costs incurred in collecting tolls are equal to about 10 per cent of the total revenue of motorway companies in France – it does not enable efficient user charging for the provision of infrastructure.

73. The cost of building a highway is 30 per cent higher than that of upgrading a trunkroad to a dual carriageway. In addition, the principle of free access to the national road network means that parallel roads have to be maintained.

74. Urban transport is discussed in more detail below.

75. At the start, British Rail suffered from the deregulation of bus services, but recaptured market shares after changing its pricing strategy.

76. Licenses covered three types of trucks depending on the maximum load capacity. Furthermore, allocation of a quota depended on distance travelled and type of good. However, there were numerous exemptions to the rules, for instance for transport on own account, or transport for public works.

77. Cost comparisons for EU countries are hampered by product heterogeneity: Dutch road hauliers, for instance, provide a wider package of services than most of their EU competitors.

78. The cost estimate for accidents is close to that of Quinet (1994).

79. It would also raise the profitability of future rail projects. It is estimated that a relative price change of 10 per cent raises profitability by ½ percentage point.

80. The most significant cut in the length of the network took place in the period 1969-73 when 3 900 km of rail-track were closed and replaced by bus services, and 400 km were closed without replacement.

81. In addition, the SNCF has suffered from an unexplained trend decline of 3 per cent per year since the mid-1980s. The shift towards road transport may be associated with the expansion and improved quality of the road network. This cannot be shown in the econometric estimates.

82. New tracks devoted to combined rail/road transports.

83. Departures were achieved by natural attrition and early retirement. Layoffs for economic reasons are not possible.

84. The SNCF itself is cross-subsidising 17 unprofitable rapid express services.

85. The age of retirement is lower than in the general social security scheme (50 years for train drivers and 55 years for all other personnel), minimum pensions are higher, pension rights are based on the last active year's earnings (as compared to the last 11 years in the general scheme) and only part of the salary forms the contribution base for paying into the system.

86. This does not give the SNCF an advantage over its competitors. On the contrary: in 1994 the rate of employer's contributions amounted to 29 per cent as compared to 14 per cent in the private sector. On the other hand, employees only pay 7 per cent as compared to 10 per cent in the private sector.

87. It is estimated that, the SNCF's deficit would have reached FF 17 billion, if its new business strategy had not been put in place at the end of 1994.

88. Given its special status, the *Ile de France* region is not representative of urban transport policies in other parts of France.

89. Draft legislation to introduce tolls on new city motorways was not passed in late 1994.

90. This implies that extensions of the current network lead to an increase in receipts for the RATP only to the extent that the number of passengers rises.

91. In contrast to the SNCF, the RATP has no contract with the State or region setting performance targets.

92. Increases in ticket prices are regulated by Ministerial decree and depend on past rises in salaries and material and energy prices. The regional administration can allow an additional 5 per cent rise in the case of an increase in supply. An even sharper rise is allowed if revenues cover less than 45 per cent of outlays.

93. On average, strikes occur twice a week and are usually wild-cat strikes on particular lines. The RATP has little clout to reduce strike activity, as it cannot fine striking workers and even has to pay them. A recent attempt to impose a minimum service obligation was not successful.

94. While current arrangements are very costly, the need to adjust could appear less urgent at the RATP as it is not suffering from inter-modal competition from liberalised sectors. This lack of competition also makes it easier for unions to capture rents.

95. In the Paris Convention (1919) signatories agreed to sovereign rights in the airspace above their territories. Civil aviation was regulated by bilateral agreements between countries. Apart from route access, sovereignty also applied to fares, frequency and capacity of flights. In recent years, fare and capacity controls have been relaxed, as bilateral agreements have been renegotiated irrespective of the EU initiative.

96. For a good review of the effects of early efforts to deregulate and introduce greater competition into the airline sector, see Chapter IV in OECD (1988a).

97. The Commission of the European Communities considered then that the financial problems of Air France could be overcome quickly and that the financial transaction was a capital injection and not a subsidy.

98. The Commission of the European Communities authorised the package under the condition that subsidies do not benefit Air Inter and that a hotel chain be sold. *CDC Participation* which is a state-dependent (but not owned) financial institution, subscribed to special bonds worth FF 1.5 billion. The Commission regarded this capital injection as a state-aid and has ordered Air France to refund it.

99. It will also need to raise funds for recapitalisation. There is little hope that the owners of Air Inter (CNAF, SNCF and Crédit Lyonnais) will be able to provide fresh capital, as they registered an overall loss of approximately FF 25 billion in 1993 and have an accumulated debt of more than FF 200 billion. Air Inter's capital has not been increased since 1980, but it has paid a cumulated FF 250 million to its shareholders. Air France, on the other hand, has received FF 3.4 billion in fresh capital since 1980 and paid FF 1 billion in dividends.

100. The cost was FF 750 000 to FF 1.3 million per docker, depending on the port.

101. Smaller ports of lesser importance are run by representatives of the Chambers of Commerce, acting as concession-holders of the infrastructure, which is owned by the State. In fact, these ports of lesser importance are more independent than the so-called ''independent ports'' (Merlin, 1994).

Bibliography

BAILY, M. (1993), "Competition, Regulation and Efficiency in Service Industries", *Brookings Papers on Economic Activity, Microeconomics*, No. 2.

BAZEN, S. and MARTIN, J. (1991), "The Impact of the Minimum Wage on Earnings and Employment in France", *OECD Economic Studies*, No. 16, Spring.

BÉRAUD, M. (1994), "Le chômage partiel, un dispositif de protection de l'emploi, comparaison dans quatre pays européens", *Travail et Emploi*, No. 61.

BORENSTEIN, S. (1992), "The Evolution of U.S. Airline Competition", *Journal of Economic Perspectives*, Vol. 6.

CINGOLANI, M. (1993), "Disparités régionales de produit par tête dans la Communauté Europénne", *EIB Papers*, No. 19 (March).

CNAV (1995), "Quelles retraites pour les salariés du secteur privé d'ici à 2015? L'étude de six carrières de référence", *Retraite et société*, No. 9/95.

Comité des Sages for Air Transport to the European Commission (1994), *Expanding Horizons*, Directorate-General for Transport, EC, Brussels.

Commissariat Général du Plan (1992), *Transports 2010*, Paris.

Commissariat Général du Plan (1993), *Transports: pour une cohérence stratégique* (report of the workshop chaired by Professor. A. Bonnafous), Paris.

Commissariat Général du Plan (1994), *Rapport Boiteux*, Paris.

CURIEN, N. and JACOBZONE, S. (1993), "Les grandes réseaux publics français de transport et de communication dans une perspective européenne", *Économie et Statistique*, No. 266, 1993-6, pp. 3-20.

EC (1994a), EC Agricultural Policy for the 21st Century, *European Economy*, No. 4, 1994.

EC (1994b), "Décision de la Commission concernant l'augmentation de capital d'Air France", *Journal officiel des Communautés européennes*, No. L 254/73.

European Conference of Ministers of Transport (1993), *Privatisation of Railways (Round Table 90)*, Paris.

European Conference of Ministers of Transport (1994a), *Transport Economics: Past Trends and Future Prospects (Round Table 100)*, Paris.

European Conference of Ministers of Transport (1994b), *Regional Policy, Transport Networks and Communications (Round Table 94)*, Paris.

FORD, R. and PORET, P. (1991), "Infrastructure and Private-sector Productivity", OECD Department of Economics and Statistics Working Papers, No. 91.

GAUTIÉ, J., GAZIER, B. and SILVERA, R. (1994). "Les subventions à l'emploi: analyses et expériences européennes", Document de Travail et Emploi, La Documentation Française.

GOOD, D.H., ADIRI, I.N., RÖLLER, L.-H. and SICKLES, R.C. (1993), "Efficiency and Productivity Growth Comparisons of European and U.S. Air Carriers: A First Look at the Data", The Journal of Productivity Analysis, Vol. 4.

GRAMLICH, E. (1994), "Infrastructure Investment: A Review Essay", Journal of Economic Literature, Vol. XXXII (September).

GRUBB, D. and WELLS, W. (1993), "Employment Regulation and Patterns of Work in EC Countries", OECD Economic Studies, No. 21, Winter.

HÖCKER, A. (1994), "La mise en oeuvre de la politique de l'emploi dans l'Union européenne", Infor MISEP No. 48.

HUART, Y. (1994), "Les effets des TGV sur l'aménagement du territoire", Note de synthèse de l'Observatoire des transports, No. 83, (September).

INFRAS/IWW (1995), External Effects of Transport, UIC, Paris.

LAGUARRIGUE, F. (1994), "Infrastructure de transport et croissance endogène", study undertaken for the ARMA, the Commissariat Général du Plan and the OEST.

Livre blanc sur les retraites (1991), La Documentation Française.

MERLIN, P. (1994), Les transports en France, La Documentation Française.

Ministère des Transports (1992), Débat national sur les structures de transport, (Rapport Carrère), Paris..

OECD (1987), Toll Financing and Private Sector Involvement in Road Infrastructure Development (available on microfiche), Paris.

OECD (1988a), Deregulation and Airline Competition, Paris.

OECD (1988b), OECD INTERLINK System: Reference Manual, Paris.

OECD (1990), Competition Policy and the Deregulation of Road Transport, Paris.

OECD (1992a), OECD Economic Surveys, France, Paris.

OECD (1992b), OECD Economic Surveys, Japan, Paris.

OECD (1995a), The Agricultural Outloook 1995-2000, Paris.

OECD (1995b), The OECD Jobs Study, Paris.

OECD (1995c), Employment Outlook, Paris.

OECD (1995d), Economic Outlook, No. 57, Paris.

OEST (1994), "Les transports en 1993", 31e Rapport de la Commission des Comptes.

OFFNER, J. M. (1993), "Les 'effets structurants' du transport: mythe politique, mystification scientifique", L'Espace géographique, No. 3.

ORR, A., EDEY, M. and KENNEDY, M. (1995), "The Determinants of Real Long-term Interest Rates: 17 Country Pooled Time Series Evidence", OECD Economics Department Working Papers, No. 155.

OSTRY, J.D. and LEVY, J. (1994), "Household Saving in France: Stochastic Income and Financial Deregulation", IMF, WP/94/136 (November).

OUM, T. and YU, C. (1994), "Economic Efficiency of Railways and Implications for Public Policy: A Comparative Study of the OECD Countries' Railways", *Journal of Transport Economics and Policy*, Vol. XXVIII, No. 2 (May).

QUINET, E. (1994), "The Social Costs of Transport: Evaluation and Links with Internalisation Policies" in *Internalising the Social Costs of Transport,* European Conference of Ministers of Transport.

RICHARDSON, P. (1988), "The Structure and Simulation Properties of OECD's INTERLINK Model", *OECD Economic Studies*, No. 10, Spring, Paris.

SOUBIE, R., PORTOS, J.L. and PRIEUR, C. (1994*), Livre blanc sur le système de santé et d'assurance maladie*, Commissariat Général du Plan, Paris.

Syndicat des Transports Parisiens (1991), *Plan stratégique des déplacements*, Paris.

TURNER, D., RICHARDSON, R. and RAUFFET, S. (1995), "Modelling the Supply Side of the Seven Major OECD Economies", Economics Department Working Papers (forthcoming).

VORNETTI, P. (1994), "The French Experience of Partnership between the Public and Private Sector in the Construction and Operation of Motorways: Theory and Practice", in OECD, *New Ways of Managing Infrastructure Provision*, Public Management Occasional Papers, No. 6.

WINSTON, C. (1991), "Efficient Transportation Infrastructure Policy", *Journal of Economic Perspectives*, Vol. 5, No. 1 (Winter).

WINSTON, C. (1993), "Economic Deregulation: Days of Reckoning for Microeconomists", *Journal of Economic Literature*, Vol. XXXI (September).

Annex I

Interest and exchange rate sensitivity of INTERLINK's French sub-model

The simulations discussed in Chapter II were conducted with the French sub-model of OECD's world macroeconomic model (Richardson, 1988, OECD, 1988*b* and Turner *et al.*, 1995). The simulation period runs from the second half of 1992 to the second half of 1995.

The first simulation concerning lower interest rates assumes that real short-term interest rates are as low as in Germany, which implies a reduction in nominal rates of some 2 percentage points on average between the second half of 1992 and the first half of 1995. In the simulation the nominal exchange rate and real government consumption and investment are held fixed, while nominal long-term rates are endogenous: as a consequence, they fall by about one percentage point below their actual value. In the model, private consumption is sensitive to real short-term interest rate changes and housing and business capital stock accumulation depend on real long-term interest rates. The long-run semi-elasticity of consumption with respect to interest rate changes is –1.3 (with no effect in the first half-year and a semi-elasticity of –0.2 in the second), that of investment is –2.6 (–0.1 in the first half year) and that of housing investment is –0.9 (–0.6 in the first half year).* Given differences in adjustment lags, a one percentage point change in interest rates over three years has the strongest effect on housing investment, followed by private consumption, and the least effect on business investment.

In the simulation, lower interest rates raise interest-rate sensitive demand components, which are further increased by higher employment and accelerator effects on business investment (Table A1). Total domestic demand is 1 per cent above its actual level in 1995, while a significant rise in imports implies a much smaller rise in real GDP. Inflation edges up somewhat, while lower interest rates reduce the government deficit.

The official French models do not include an interest rate effect and their response to an interest rate change is smaller than that of the OECD's model. Estimation of the OECD's consumption function revealed that the magnitude of the interest-rate coefficient increased substantially in the early 1980s and remained rather stable at a higher level

---

* Residential and business investment are not modelled directly, but change with respect to desired levels of the housing and business sector capital stocks. While an interest rate change changes the growth of stocks permanently, the effect on the growth of flows is transitory. The transition is fairly short for housing investment, but long for business investment.

Table A1. **Simulation of lower interest rates**

Differences from baseline levels in per cent

	1992	1993	1994	1995
Private consumption	0.0	0.6	0.9	1.2
Residential construction	0.0	0.9	1.7	1.9
Business investment	0.0	1.4	2.0	2.1
Total domestic demand	0.0	0.6	1.0	1.1
Foreign balance [1]	0.0	−0.3	−0.5	−0.7
Real GDP	0.0	0.4	0.5	0.5
Consumer price level	0.0	0.1	0.4	0.7
Rate of inflation [2]	0.0	0.1	0.3	0.3
Interest rates [3]				
Real short-term	−1.2	−3.1	−1.5	−1.3
Real long-term	−0.3	−1.3	−1.1	−1.2
Government deficit [4]	0.2	0.8	0.8	1.2
Current account [4]	0.0	−0.3	−0.5	−0.6

1. As a per cent of GDP in the previous period.
2. Difference in percentage points.
3. Change in level.
4. Change in level as a percentage of GDP.
Source: OECD.

Table A2. **Simulation of lower exchange rates**

Differences from baseline levels in per cent

	1992	1993	1994	1995
Private consumption	−0.1	−0.1	−0.2	−0.4
Residential construction	0.1	0.6	1.6	2.9
Business investment	0.3	2.0	3.1	3.7
Total domestic demand	0.0	0.3	0.5	0.5
Foreign balance [1]	0.1	0.4	0.6	0.8
Real GDP	0.1	0.7	1.0	1.3
Consumer price level	0.1	0.6	1.5	2.9
Rate of inflation [2]	0.1	0.5	0.9	1.4
Interest rates [3]				
Real short-term	−0.2	−0.6	−1.0	−1.6
Real long-term	−0.2	−0.6	−1.0	−1.6
Government deficit [4]	0.0	0.1	0.3	0.5
Current account [4]	0.0	0.1	0.3	0.5

1. As a per cent of GDP in the previous period.
2. Difference in percentage points.
3. Change in level.
4. Change in level as a percentage of GDP.
Source: OECD.

thereafter. The response of INTERLINK's French sub-model to interest rate changes is still smaller over the short-run than the sub-models for Germany or the United Kingdom, presumably reflecting the fact that French households are large net creditors.

In the second simulation, a fall in the nominal effective exchange rate is assumed as a consequence of lower interest rates. The latter are not simulated in order to clearly distinguish the interest rate from the exchange rate sensitivity of the model and interest rates are held constant in nominal terms. As short-run exchange rate behaviour is difficult to model, an exchange rate path was imposed, with the exchange rate falling initially by three per cent and then a further one per cent per half-year, so that the exchange rate is close to 10 per cent below its baseline value in 1995. In this simulation, exports rise substantially, which also raises business investment (Table A2). On the other hand, the lower exchange rate raises the rate of inflation significantly and lowers private consumption. The simulation highlights the short-run growth-inflation trade-off of a permanently lower nominal exchange rate.

Such simulation results strongly depend on the assumed exchange rate path and assumptions about the reaction of the monetary authorities and international investors to higher inflation. Over the long-run (about 10 years) the model shows no output gains following a devaluation, as competitiveness gains are lost due to higher inflation, and a change in the price level proportionate to the devaluation.

Annex II

Calendar of main economic events

FISCAL POLICY

1994

March

The 1993 budget deficit amounted to FF 315.7 billion, or 4.5 per cent of GDP.

In 1993, the general government debt according to the Maastricht definition was 44.9 per cent of GDP, compared with 39.5 per cent in 1992.

April

The letter sent by the Prime Minister to the various ministries setting out spending guidelines for the 1995 budget recommended that operating expenditure be cut by 8 per cent and that intervention expenditure not committed by the State be reduced by 15 per cent. The aim is to cut the deficit to FF 275 billion in 1995, as against a projected FF 300 billion for 1994.

September

The Government presents its draft Budget for 1995. The deficit is to be reduced to FF 301.4 billion in 1994 and FF 274.6 billion in 1995. Priority will be given to social expenditure, employment and the fight against exclusion. Revenue will rise by 4.7 per cent to FF 1 208.7 billion, and the increase in expenditure will limited to 1.9 per cent in line with projected inflation. FF 55 billion are expected from privatisations. The Budget is based on the assumption of real GDP growth of 3.1 per cent.

December

The National Assembly adopts the 1995 draft budget with very few amendments (a deficit of FF 275.1 billion, or 3.6 per cent of GDP).

1995

January

The tax on petroleum products is raised, and the standard rate of VAT on horticultural products is replaced by the lower rate.

July

Amendments to the State Budget include several spending initiatives in favour of employment, the housing sector and small and medium-sized enterprises. A rise in taxation will cover these initiatives, as well as overspending and revenue shortfalls in the first half of the year. The deficit (adjusted for accounting changes) will remain unchanged from that projected in the initial 1995 Budget.

MONETARY POLICY

1994

January

Banks cut their base rate from 8.15 per cent to 7.95 per cent.

The Council of Ministers decides the composition of the Monetary Policy Council. The term of office (three, six and nine years) of each member of the Council was drawn by lot.

The Monetary Policy Council sets its targets for 1994. The final target is inflation of below 2 per cent, which presupposes the continued pursuit of the intermediate objectives – the stability of the franc in the European exchange rate mechanism and medium-term growth of 5 per cent of M3 and total domestic debt.

February

The *Banque de France* lowers its tender rate from 6.20 to 6.10 per cent.

March

The *Banque de France* lowers its tender rate from 6.10 to 5.90 per cent in two steps.

April

The *Banque de France* lowers its tender rate from 5.90 to 5.60 per cent in three steps. It lowers its 5-10 day repurchase rate from 7 to 6.75 per cent.

May

The *Banque de France* cuts its tender rate from 5.70 to 5.40 per cent in three steps. It lowers the 5-10 day repurchase rate from 6.75 to 6.40 per cent.

Banks cut their base rate from 7.95 to 7.70 per cent.

June

The *Banque de France* lowers its tender rate from 5.40 to 5.10 per cent.

July

The *Banque de France* lowers its tender rate from 5.10 to 5 per cent.

December

The *Banque de France* sets targets of growth of 5 per cent for M3 and of inflation below 2 per cent. These are the same as in 1994.

March

The *Banque de France* suspends the 5-10 day repurchase facility and replaces it by a 24-hour lending facility at 8 per cent.

April

The *Banque de France* lowers its 24-hour repurchase rate from 8 to 7.75 per cent.

OTHER MEASURES

1994

January

Measures increasing the length of pension contributions and modifying the method of calculation of the reference salary for the basic pension come into force.

The European Commission decides to take the French Government to the Court of Justice in Luxembourg on the grounds that it has maintained its monopoly on gas and electricity, despite its undertakings in 1991.

The European Commission blocks the payment of State aid of FF 2.5 billion to the Bull group and starts an investigation into all the capital injections the company has received since February 1993.

Measures to bolster activity and promote employment are announced:

– employees to be allowed to withdraw in advance their participation in profit-sharing schemes in order to buy a new car or to carry out major home renovation work;
– a subsidy of FF 5 000 to be paid for taking a vehicle over 10 years old off the road and purchasing a new car, the ceiling on the depreciation of company cars to be raised;
– rate of interest on home-purchase saving accounts and plans, and the rates on loans attached to them, to be lowered;
– reimbursement of VAT to be speeded up by a month for companies that take on and train young people;
– job and vocational training subsidies announced in spring 1993 to be extended to end-1994;
– FF 100 million to be made available for identifying potential sources of jobs.

February

Creation of a special short-term financing facility of FF 300 million, provided by the *Caisse française de développement*, to help firms overcome cash-flow difficulties resulting from the devaluation of the CFA franc.

Launch of the ELF-Aquitaine privatisation: 33 million shares offered at a unit price of FF 385. Ninety-eight million share applications are received from the public.

The Ministry of Agriculture and Fisheries announces a FF 300 million package for the fisheries sector, including FF 150 million for rescheduling subsidised loans to firms in difficulty. Also, fishermen's social insurance contributions halved until 1 June 1994.

Renault sells part of its stake in the Volvo AB group following the cancellation of its planned merger with the Swedish group, realising a capital gain of FF 750 million.

Announcement of state aid of FF 2 billion to *Aérospatiale*.

The agreement reached between the social partners on balancing the pension scheme for managerial staff (*Association générale des institutions des retraités cadres* – AGIRC) confirmed the freeze of pensions in 1994, introduced a pensioners' solidarity contribution, and set out a timetable for raising the compulsory rate of employer and employee contributions.

The Government brings forward by five years the opening date for about 2 600 km of motorway, representing an investment of FF 140 billion. Also, the motorway companies to be grouped into three regional entities in order to strengthen their finances and improve their management.

March

The rescue plan for Air France, which was submitted to each employee of the company and the unions, provides for a massive capital injection (at least FF 20 billion), 5 000 redundancies over three years (12 per cent of the workforce), a wage freeze, and the opening up of 15 per cent of the capital to employees in return for wage concessions and a complete overhaul of the company's organisation.

Presentation of the rescue plan for *Crédit Lyonnais* following the losses incurred in 1993 (FF 6.9 billion). A capital increase to be provided, of which FF 3.5 billion from the State, FF 1.2 billion from Thomson and FF 200 million from the *Caisse des dépôts et consignations*. A special vehicle to be set up to take over FF 40 billion of property loans, of which FF 18.4 billion will be guaranteed by the State. In return, the bank will dispose of FF 20 billion of assets and slash its overheads drastically.

Following the suspension of the FF 2.5 billion advance on the capital injection into Bull, as requested by the European Commission, the Government announces that the group will be privatised. Two state-owned insurance companies, UAP and AGF, are also to be privatised rapidly.

April

The subsidy for hiring young people (FF 1 000 per month), initially introduced for nine months, to be continued for five years.

The Prime Minister announces two new measures to stimulate consumption: the measure allowing employees to withdraw their participation from profit-sharing schemes to be extended, and the tripling of the school-start allowance in 1994 to be repeated.

Launch of the UAP privatisation. Shares priced at FF 152, *i.e.* 7.3 per cent less than the last quoted price. This sale, which concerned 50.2 per cent of the capital held by the State, was to have brought in some FF 18.5 billion.

The Ministry of Finance announces a cut of one point, to 6.75 per cent, in the rate of ordinary loans by the Economic and Social Development Fund, in order to help firms in difficulty.

Further to a complaint lodged by the European Commission, the French authorities are ordered to open up air routes from Orly to London, Toulouse and Marseille, to foreign airlines.

May

The Government authorises a package of FF 325 million for training drivers and modernising road haulage companies.

The National Assembly adopts a bill on supplementary social protection for wage-earners, which transposes two EC insurance directives into the French social security code.

The Council of Ministers adopts a social security bill which increases the independence of the four branches of the general scheme and clarifies their financial relationship with the State.

June

The Council of Ministers adopts the draft guideline Act on territorial development. The government widens priority rural areas, which henceforth include 13 million people, and announces measures to promote rural development embracing economic activities, public services and housing.

The Ministry of Agriculture announces measures to make it easier for young farmers to start up, and tax relief of some FF 500 million for cereal producers through cuts in several specific taxes.

The Government announces that the payment times of the State and public entities are to be shortened to 40 days as from 1 August and to 35 days as from 1 January of the following year, compared with 45 days at present.

In application of the law, the Government decides to raise the hourly rate of the SMIC by 2.1 per cent as from 1 July, bringing it up to FF 35.56, or a gross monthly wage of FF 6 009.64

Adoption of a social security bill which establishes the financial independence of the four branches of the general scheme and increases Parliament's powers of oversight.

July

The Council of Ministers adopts a decree increasing the term of appointment of the chairmen of public enterprises from 3 to 5 years.

Publication of the report by the parliamentary commission of inquiry into *Crédit Lyonnais*.

The Ministry of Industry asks EDF-GDF to withdraw from four sectors (intelligent homes, cartography, remote monitoring and waste collection) and sets up a structure to monitor its policy of diversification.

The European Commission gives its agreement, subject to certain conditions, to the recapitalisation of Air France.

August

The Ministry of Agriculture announces a reduction in farmers' social insurance contributions of 9 per cent on average in 1994 compared with 1993, financed by an additional allocation of FF 120 million from central government.

Pensions of farmers raised by 10 per cent, retroactive from 1 January, at a cost of FF 500 million to central government.

The Minister of Justice presents a bill to the Cabinet of Ministers to bring French legislation into line with the provisions of the Council of Europe Convention on 8 November last on "laundering, search, seizure and confiscation of the proceeds from crime". The notion of money laundering is extended to all capital of unlawful origin, including that resulting from tax evasion.

September

Publication of a decree authorising the professions to deduct contributions to funded supplementary pension schemes from their taxable income.

The Government announces the launch of a new programme to transfer 10 000 public sector jobs from Paris to the regions.

October

The ceiling on the Codevi is raised from FF 20 000 to FF 30 000.

According to the social security audit commission, the social security deficit is set to attain FF 54.4 billion in 1994 and FF 50.5 billion in 1995; exemptions from employer contributions which are not offset by central government will cost the social security system FF 13.5 billion in 1995.

The Minister for Social Affairs states that the Government's objective is to provide over 40 per cent of the 700 000 recipients of the guaranteed minimum income (RMI) with a job or training next year, at a cost of FF 7 billion.

The European Commission gives its approval to the FF 11.1 billion capital injection for restructuring Bull prior to its privatisation.

November

The public offering of Renault shares brought in nearly FF 8 billion to the State, raising the total proceeds from privatisations since early 1994 to FF 60 billion.

In its report to Parliament on the future of the compulsory basic social security schemes, the Government projects that their accounts will be in balance in 1997, following deficits of FF 28 billion in 1996 and FF 50.4 billion in 1995.

December

The provision allowing employees to draw funds out of profit-sharing schemes in order to finance major home renovation work is extended for 6 months.

The Government and the state-owned insurance group AGF decide measures to restructure one of the group's subsidiaries with a view to privatising AGF.

The State gives Air France a capital injection of FF 5 billion, bringing to FF 8.2 billion the amount paid in 1994 out of the FF 10 billion scheduled.

The Government authorises TAT (British Airways), AOM (a subsidiary of *Crédit Lyonnais*) and Air Liberté to compete as from 1 January 1995 on the Orly-Marseille and Orly-Toulouse routes.

Publication of a White Paper on the health and sickness insurance system, commissioned by the Prime Minister from three experts.

1995

January

An agreement is signed between the doctors' unions and the *Caisse Nationale d'assurance-maladie* on spending targets for ambulatory medicine (up by 3 per cent) in 1995 and on fee increases.

Old-age and disability pensions, and family allowances, raised by 1.2 per cent on 1 January 1995.

Guaranteed minimum income (RMI) raised by 1.2 per cent on 1 January 1995.

Parliament adopts a bill on the modernisation of agriculture.

Employer contributions to the pension scheme for local authority employees raised by 3.8 percentage points.

The rate for subsidised home lease-purchase loans (*prêts locatifs*) cut from 5.8 to 4.8 per cent, and a government subsidy amounting to as much as 25 per cent of the cost of construction is planned.

February

Promulgation of the Guideline Act on land use and territorial development.

Privatisation of the state tobacco company (SEITA).

March

Measures adopted to boost the housing market (10 000 loans for first-time buyers) and small business.

Announcement of a second rescue package for *Crédit Lyonnais*, which provides in particular for the transfer of FF 135 billion of assets to a special structure underwritten by the State, which will be responsible for selling them, and a refocusing of the bank's business.

May

Privatisation of Usinor-Sacilor announced.

The SNCF is authorised to lease out its telecommunications network.

The new Government announces its programme, which provides new employment programmes, an increase of 4 per cent in the SMIC on 1 July 1995, and an increase in old-age pensions and the standard rate of VAT.

STATISTICAL ANNEX AND STRUCTURAL INDICATORS

Table A. Selected background statistics

	Average 1985-94	1985	1986	1987	1988	1989	1990	1991	1992	1993	1994
A. Percentage changes from previous year											
Private consumption[1]	2.3	2.4	3.9	2.9	3.3	3.1	2.7	1.4	1.4	0.2	1.5
Gross fixed capital formation[1]	2.5	3.2	4.5	4.8	9.6	7.9	2.8	0.0	-3.1	-5.8	1.4
General government	5.0	9.8	3.2	3.3	13.8	6.5	0.7	5.4	4.0	-0.3	3.3
Residential construction	0.5	-2.1	1.3	3.3	7.1	7.1	0.3	-4.1	-4.2	-6.7	2.5
Private non-residential	2.9	4.4	6.6	6.0	9.6	8.6	4.7	0.4	-4.6	-7.1	0.3
GDP[1]	2.1	1.9	2.5	2.3	4.5	4.3	2.5	0.8	1.3	-1.5	2.8
Deflators:											
GDP	3.2	5.8	5.2	3.0	2.8	3.0	3.1	3.3	2.1	2.5	1.3
Exports of goods and services	0.7	4.7	-3.0	-0.5	2.6	4.8	-1.3	0.7	-1.6	-1.5	1.9
Imports of goods and services	-0.7	2.0	-12.7	-0.6	2.5	6.6	-1.3	0.0	-2.4	-2.7	1.7
Total domestic demand	2.9	5.2	2.9	2.8	2.7	3.3	3.0	3.1	2.0	2.5	1.1
Industrial production	1.3	0.2	0.9	1.9	4.7	4.1	1.9	0.0	-1.0	-3.6	4.0
Employment	0.3	-0.1	0.5	0.4	1.0	1.4	1.0	0.0	-0.7	-1.2	0.5
Compensation of employees (current prices)	4.7	6.4	5.0	4.3	5.5	6.4	6.6	4.8	3.8	1.5	2.5
Productivity (GDP[1]/employment)	1.8	2.0	2.0	1.8	3.4	2.8	1.5	0.8	2.0	-0.3	2.3
Unit labour costs (compensation/GDP)[1]	2.5	4.4	2.4	2.0	1.0	2.0	4.0	4.0	2.4	3.0	-0.3
B. Percentages ratios											
Gross fixed capital formation as a per cent of GDP at constant prices	21.4	20.0	20.4	20.9	21.9	22.7	22.8	22.6	21.6	20.7	20.4
Stockbuilding as a per cent of GDP at constant prices	0.4	-0.1	0.7	0.8	0.9	1.2	1.3	0.5	0.2	-1.7	-0.1
Foreign balance as a per cent of GDP at constant prices	-1.2	0.9	-1.0	-2.1	-2.3	-1.9	-2.1	-1.9	-0.9	-0.1	-0.3
Compensation of employees as a per cent of GDP at current prices	52.4	54.7	53.3	52.8	51.8	51.3	51.8	52.1	52.3	52.5	51.7
Direct taxes as a per cent of household income	6.7	6.6	6.7	6.7	6.4	6.3	6.2	6.9	6.9	7.0	7.2
Household saving as a per cent of disposable income	12.7	14.0	12.9	10.8	11.0	11.7	12.5	13.2	13.7	13.8	13.4
Unemployment as a per cent of civilian labour force	10.3	10.2	10.4	10.5	10.0	9.4	8.9	9.4	10.3	11.7	12.4
C. Other indicator											
Current balance (billion US dollars)	-0.6	-0.3	1.8	-5.0	-4.8	-4.7	-9.8	-6.1	3.9	9.2	9.8

1. At constant 1980 prices.
Source: OECD estimates.

Table B. Gross domestic product and expenditure
FF billion

	1985	1986	1987	1988	1989	1990	1991	1992	1993	1994
	Current prices									
Private consumption	2 858.4	3 049.5	3 235.6	3 429.5	3 655.8	3 861.3	4 037.5	4 189.8	4 291.6	4 433.6
Public consumption	923.0	972.8	1 018.6	1 073.3	1 122.0	1 187.7	1 257.1	1 339.1	1 423.9	1 460.9
Gross fixed capital formation	905.3	977.5	1 054.8	1 188.3	1 314.6	1 391.4	1 436.9	1 401.9	1 319.2	1 347.3
Change in stocks	–17.9	17.2	20.7	40.3	59.3	70.9	21.0	–14.9	–106.5	–23.8
Domestic expenditure	4 668.8	5 017.0	5 329.6	5 731.4	6 151.6	6 511.3	6 752.6	6 916.0	6 928.2	7 218.0
Exports of goods and services	1 123.9	1 074.1	1 101.4	1 221.3	1 411.1	1 468.0	1 538.1	1 587.9	1 558.7	1 681.3
less: Imports of goods and services	1 092.6	1 021.8	1 094.3	1 217.6	1 403.1	1 469.8	1 514.5	1 493.4	1 404.2	1 522.5
Gross domestic product at market prices	4 700.2	5 069.3	5 336.6	5 735.1	6 159.7	6 509.5	6 776.2	7 010.5	7 082.8	7 376.9
	1980 prices									
Private consumption	1 814.9	1 886.0	1 939.9	2 003.0	2 064.3	2 120.0	2 148.7	2 178.0	2 182.3	2 214.6
Public consumption	584.1	594.1	610.9	631.9	634.9	648.3	666.4	689.3	712.1	719.5
Gross fixed capital formation	605.9	633.2	663.8	727.4	784.7	807.0	807.4	782.6	737.2	747.5
of which:										
Corporate, quasi-corporate and private unincorporated enterprises	314.7	334.5	354.1	387.8	422.8	441.2	441.5	427.9	401.1	401.0
Households	175.5	177.7	183.6	196.5	210.5	211.2	202.6	194.1	181.1	185.6
General government	98.7	101.9	105.3	119.9	127.7	128.6	135.5	140.9	140.5	145.2
Non-profit organisations, credit institutions and insurance companies	17.1	19.1	20.8	23.2	23.7	26.1	27.9	19.7	14.5	15.7
Change in stocks	–2.6	23.3	26.3	30.5	40.0	45.7	19.2	5.5	–59.7	–2.4
Domestic expenditure	3 002.3	3 136.6	3 240.9	3 392.8	3 523.8	3 621.0	3 641.7	3 655.3	3 571.8	3 679.1
Exports of goods and services	696.5	686.4	707.4	764.6	842.6	887.7	924.1	969.3	965.9	1 022.2
less: Imports of goods and services	670.4	718.3	773.7	840.1	908.0	963.6	993.0	1 003.7	969.9	1 033.5
Gross domestic product at market prices	3 028.4	3 104.6	3 174.5	3 317.3	3 458.4	3 545.1	3 572.8	3 620.9	3 567.9	3 667.8

Source: OECD, *Annual National Accounts.*

Table C. **The money supply and its counterparts**

FF billion, end of period

	1985	1986	1987	1988	1989	1990	1991	1992	1993	1994
Money supply										
A. M1	1 296.3	1 388.9	1 449	1 508.6	1 634.5	1 697.8	1 618.9	1 607.1	1 629.4	1 677.8
of which:										
Sight deposits	1 090.5	1 176.6	1 227.2	1 273	1 388	1 442.4	1 364.5	1 351.6	1 376.9	1 425.4
B. M2	2 473.4	2 587.7	2 699.1	2 798.9	2 930.5	2 956.3	2 858	2 810.8	2 858	3 009.5
of which:										
Livrets A and livrets bleus	761.3	760.6	788.5	806.2	802.1	789.2	768.9	740.7	737.4	774
C. M3	3 322.1	3 547.4	3 894.7	4 219.1	4 623.6	5 034.3	5 160.3	5 316.2	5 165.4	5 281.2
of which:										
Time deposits and paper denominated in francs	822.1	934.9	1 168	1 369.1	1 600.6	2 015.7	2 248.2	2 442.5	2 225.8	2 186.5
D. M4	3 325.2	3 570.2	3 934.3	4 259.5	4 686.3	5 083.9	5 209.4	5 371.8	5 214.1	5 349.5
Counterparts[1]										
A. External	66.5	154.1	127.1	80.7	54.5	–50.2	–40.3	240.2	628.1	452.9
B. Claims on Treasury	815.3	911.1	930	1 024	970.8	974.3	1 014.2	1 091.9	1 353.3	1 723.7
Loans and advances by the Banque de France	23.6	25.3	36.5	36.9	28.9	38.5	26.4	40.8	36	24
Other credit institutions	152.5	159.8	176.5	166.5	173.8	172.4	156.7	154.4	152.6	144.9
C. Domestic lending	4 137.3	4 593.5	5 105	5 767.3	6 516.4	7 084	7 393.3	7 810.9	7 698.3	7 502.6
D. Long term financing (–)	1 276.3	1 685.5	1 812.7	2 139	2 412.5	2 410.9	2 586.3	2 809.3	3 381.6	3 355.3
E. Contractual savings and PEP[2] (–)	236.8	295.4	351.3	408.7	448.6	538.6	624.8	703.3	861.9	920.2
F. Miscellaneous, net	–193.9	–180	–103.3	–105.3	–56.9	–24.3	4.3	–152	–63.2	–97.7

1. The figures for 1994 are those for June.
2. Plans d'épargne populaire.
Source: Banque de France.

Table D. **Balance of payments on a transactions basis**

$ million[1]

	1985	1986	1987	1988	1989	1990	1991	1992	1993	1994
Exports (fob)	95 225	118 613	140 803	159 971	171 096	206 820	207 712	226 523	198 636	222 320
Imports (fob)	100 588	121 375	150 040	168 433	181 168	219 735	216 536	223 636	189 939	212 438
Trade balance	-5 363	-2 762	-9 237	-8 462	-10 072	-12 915	-8 824	2 887	8 697	9 882
Services, net	3 966	4 481	4 202	4 604	7 127	4 250	3 111	2 303	1 320	2 740
of which:										
Major works projects	1 329	936	1 167	719	707	1 172	1 370	1 761	1 481	1 501
Travel	3 385	3 211	3 378	4 071	6 214	7 927	9 043	11 278	10 727	10 881
Investment income	-1 553	-487	-408	60	478	-2 958	-5 069	-7 737	-8 081	-9 600
Other goods and services, net	3 699	4 696	5 395	5 786	5 832	6 985	6 923	7 580	5 345	5 232
Private transfers, net	-1 295	-1 735	-2 298	-2 430	-1 907	-2 770	-2 555	-3 213	-688	-819
Official transfers, net	-1 336	-2 845	-3 052	-4 332	-5 657	-5 385	-4 776	-5 687	-5 423	-7 239
Current balance	-329	1 835	-4 990	-4 834	-4 677	-9 835	-6 121	3 870	9 251	9 796
Long-term capital	3 265	-7 793	2 190	-632	10 738	15 152	1 714	22 702	-4 215	-46 635
Private	7 035	-1 117	7 519	4 202	15 295	17 491	6 705	26 930	-996	-48 011
Official	-3 770	-6 676	-5 329	-4 834	-4 557	-2 339	-4 991	-4 228	-3 219	1 376
Basic balance	2 936	-5 958	-2 800	-5 466	6 061	5 317	-4 407	26 572	5 036	-36 839
Short-term capital	2 166	4 665	3 610	2 206	-15 940	-17 704	-1 791	-1 913	39 931	4 321
Balance of non-monetary transactions	5 102	-1 293	810	-3 260	-9 879	-12 387	-6 198	24 659	44 967	-32 518
Bank capital	-2 826	2 986	-9 299	2 343	5 805	27 427	755	-45 389	-49 831	49 215
Balance on official settlements	2 276	1 693	-8 489	-917	-4 074	15 040	-5 443	-20 730	-4 864	16 697
Net position with FECOM	0	24	3 913	-3 984	0	0	0	0	4 130	-4 133
Miscellaneous assets and liabilities	476	14	1 980	-405	3 353	-4 199	395	19 480	-4 717	-10 131
Change in official reserves	2 752	1 731	-2 596	-5 306	-721	10 841	-5 048	-1 250	-5 451	2 433

1. Exchange rate 1985: $1 = 8.984; 1986: $1 = 6.927; 1987: $1 = 6.009; 1988: $1 = 5.956; 1989: $1 = 6.380; 1990: $1 = 5.446; 1991: $1 = 5.641; 1992: $1 = 5.294; 1993: $1 = 5.662; 1994: $1 = 5.552.

Source: OECD.

Table E. **Foreign trade by commodity**

	Structure (in % of total)		Percentage change from previous year						
	1986	1993	1987	1988	1989	1990	1991	1992	1993
Exports, fob	100.0	100.0	20.2	13.0	6.7	21.4	1.6	8.7	-6.8
SITC classification									
0. Food and live animals	12.0	12.3	14.9	17.3	5.8	19.0	-0.8	12.3	-1.8
1. Beverage and tobacco	3.5	3.2	23.5	9.4	6.8	22.2	-1.1	5.7	-7.6
2. Crude materials, inedible, except fuels	3.6	2.3	29.6	18.1	-0.8	1.5	-13.1	-0.2	-16.0
3. Mineral fuels, lubricants and related materials	2.8	2.8	-0.7	2.8	14.2	30.4	9.6	0.0	8.4
4. Animal and vegetable oils and fats	0.2	0.2	1.8	29.3	17.1	3.7	-1.7	9.1	-9.8
5. Chemical products	14.1	14.2	21.9	15.2	1.3	18.4	1.8	9.0	-1.9
6. Other manufactured goods classified chiefly by material	18.6	16.1	16.3	14.2	8.9	15.2	-2.4	6.3	-9.5
7. Machinery and transport equipment	34.8	38.4	22.6	12.0	8.3	27.2	5.9	9.9	-9.1
8. Miscellaneous manufactured articles	10.0	10.4	24.1	11.8	5.6	27.1	-0.6	9.8	-6.4
9. Other	0.4	0.1	25.1	-69.2	148.5	-42.6	-22.3	-5.8	-25.2
Imports, cif	100.0	100.0	23.2	12.2	7.6	22.3	-1.0	3.5	-12.1
SITC classification									
0. Food and live animals	10.1	9.5	17.2	8.2	1.4	16.8	5.3	5.4	-7.8
1. Beverage and tobacco	1.0	1.2	19.2	16.6	4.9	22.9	4.5	7.8	-1.7
2. Crude materials, inedible, except fuels	4.6	3.2	19.5	15.6	8.0	5.0	-9.9	0.1	-19.4
3. Mineral fuels, lubricants and related materials	12.7	8.9	4.9	-14.1	15.7	32.3	0.1	-7.9	-9.2
4. Animal and vegetable oils and fats	0.4	0.3	-6.8	16.5	8.2	14.6	-4.2	0.1	0.2
5. Chemical products	10.7	11.4	23.2	15.6	5.6	20.5	-2.5	8.2	-8.7
6. Other manufactured goods classified chiefly by material	17.8	15.8	20.7	17.6	8.4	18.8	-7.4	2.7	-16.7
7. Machinery and transport equipment	29.6	34.5	31.9	18.0	8.2	24.9	0.6	4.1	-13.1
8. Miscellaneous manufactured articles	13.0	15.1	31.8	11.2	5.9	25.1	2.3	6.7	-10.2
9. Other	0.1	0.0	50.1	17.7	23.2	-7.2	7.1	-7.4	-49.3

Source: OECD, *Foreign Trade Statistics*, Series C.

Table F. Foreign trade by origin

	Structure (in % of total)		Percentage change from previous year						
	1987	1994	1988	1989	1990	1991	1992	1993	1994
Exports, fob									
World	100.0	100.0	12.2	7.4	21.3	1.9	8.7	-10.4	12.4
OECD	79.3	78.9	14.3	6.2	22.3	1.8	7.8	-12.2	13.4
EC	63.4	63.3	14.4	7.0	23.3	1.7	8.2	-14.0	14.1
of which:									
Germany	16.9	17.2	10.3	5.9	29.2	8.8	2.5	-11.3	11.0
Belgium-Luxembourg	9.3	8.8	8.8	5.6	28.0	-1.4	10.4	-15.3	13.4
Italy	12.1	9.4	13.9	6.0	13.9	-1.3	7.5	-22.6	12.2
Netherlands	5.1	4.6	23.9	8.3	20.7	-10.1	6.9	-11.2	7.8
United Kingdom	8.8	9.9	24.3	4.9	18.3	-2.4	12.8	-8.5	18.1
United States	7.3	7.0	12.9	-3.9	12.8	6.1	11.6	-2.4	11.5
Japan	1.5	2.0	24.0	19.8	23.5	7.3	-3.5	-3.0	13.1
Non-OECD	20.6	21.0	4.3	13.0	17.2	1.9	12.6	-3.4	8.7
COMECON	2.0	1.7	11.2	-2.9	-0.5	22.4	39.6	-31.0	11.0
OPEC	4.3	3.5	-4.8	11.7	26.4	1.2	16.6	-10.4	-7.3
Other	14.3	15.9	6.1	15.6	17.0	0.0	8.1	3.2	12.7
Unspecified	0.1	0.1	-50.3	-62.5	33.9	15.9	132.1	131.9	-8.4
Imports, cif									
World	100.0	100.0	11.3	8.3	22.4	-0.9	3.6	-15.3	13.2
OECD	81.4	80.5	11.6	8.0	21.8	-1.5	3.9	-16.1	14.1
EC	64.5	62.6	10.1	7.8	21.4	-3.2	5.6	-16.8	15.0
of which:									
Germany	20.0	17.8	11.2	6.4	18.5	-6.1	7.5	-20.0	14.3
Belgium-Luxembourg	9.4	9.1	8.6	8.8	17.4	-5.1	5.7	-12.3	15.9
Italy	11.7	10.1	10.9	6.9	22.8	-6.1	0.6	-20.7	14.9
Netherlands	5.6	5.0	2.4	8.4	19.8	0.8	1.9	-14.1	9.9
United Kingdom	7.1	8.0	14.5	6.3	24.3	3.8	5.0	-11.6	12.6
United States	7.2	8.5	19.8	8.1	29.5	11.7	-5.3	-12.3	10.9
Japan	3.8	3.7	22.1	6.7	19.0	1.8	2.8	-15.0	2.6
Non-OECD	17.3	18.1	7.9	9.5	24.1	3.3	1.0	-9.1	9.2
COMECON	2.6	1.4	5.4	-1.7	24.1	-5.3	13.4	-52.5	19.7
OPEC	4.4	3.7	-12.2	29.4	30.4	3.6	-11.0	-9.7	-0.8
Other	10.3	13.0	17.1	5.8	21.6	5.0	3.6	0.4	11.3
Unspecified	1.4	1.4	35.6	9.1	33.4	-9.5	15.4	-36.9	14.9

Source: OECD, *Foreign Trade Statistics*, Series A.

155

Table G. **Structure of output and performance indicators**

A. Structure of output (constant prices)

	Share of GDP						Share of total employment					
	1980	1985	1990	1992	1993	1994	1980	1985	1990	1992	1993	1994
Agriculture, hunting, forestry and fishing	4.6	5.0	4.6	4.7	4.3	4.3	8.6	7.2	5.6	5.2	5.0	4.8
Mining and quarrying	2.4	2.1	1.6	1.6	1.7	1.5	0.6	0.5	0.3	0.3	0.3	0.3
Manufacturing	25.1	22.9	22.3	21.4	20.7	21.1	24.5	22.3	20.4	19.6	18.8	18.3
of which:												
Food products	3.5	3.3	3.0	2.9	3.0	3.0	2.7	2.8	2.6	2.5	2.5	2.5
Textiles	1.8	1.6	1.3	1.2	1.1	1.1	2.6	2.1	1.7	1.5	1.4	1.3
Paper	0.6	0.6	0.5	0.5	0.4	0.4	0.5	0.5	0.5	0.5	0.5	0.5
Chemicals	2.1	2.3	2.5	2.6	2.7	2.7	1.5	1.4	1.4	1.3	1.3	1.3
Metals	1.3	1.1	1.1	1.0	1.0	1.1	1.1	0.9	0.7	0.6	0.6	0.5
Metal products, machinery and equipment	8.4	7.7	7.7	7.4	6.9	7.1	8.3	7.6	6.9	6.7	6.4	6.2
Electricity, gas and water	2.0	2.7	2.6	2.7	2.8	2.8	0.7	0.8	0.7	0.7	0.7	0.7
Construction	7.6	6.5	6.8	6.4	6.1	5.8	8.5	7.3	7.4	7.1	6.9	6.7
Traded services[1]	40.8	42.8	45.3	46.0	46.7	46.6	35.2	37.2	40.5	40.9	40.9	41.5
Non-traded services	17.5	18.0	16.8	17.2	17.8	17.9	21.9	24.8	25.0	26.2	27.3	27.8
Total traded goods and services	82.5	82.0	83.2	82.8	82.2	82.1	78.1	75.2	75.0	73.8	72.7	72.2

B. Economic performance (constant prices)

	Productivity growth[2]						Share of total investment					
	1980	1985	1990	1992	1993	1994	1980	1985	1990	1992	1993	1994
Agriculture, hunting, forestry and fishing	7.2	7.2	7.0	11.5	-3.8	5.9	3.6	3.3	2.8	2.3	2.3	2.5
Mining and quarrying	1.8	-1.7	4.9	9.0	6.8	-2.9	1.7	1.3	1.0	0.9	1.0	1.0
Manufacturing	2.0	1.6	1.3	3.3	0.1	7.6	13.8	14.4	15.6	15.0	12.8	12.6
of which:												
Food products	-0.2	2.7	1.4	-1.2	4.7	3.0	2.0	2.4	2.3	2.8	2.0	1.9
Textiles	3.7	1.5	6.8	7.3	1.6	5.5	0.6	0.7	0.6	0.4	0.4	0.3
Paper	2.9	-2.2	-0.2	0.7	-8.8	12.5	0.4	0.4	0.7	0.8	0.6	0.6
Chemicals	5.6	0.2	4.5	8.7	4.9	4.1	1.4	1.4	1.6	1.8	1.7	1.6
Metals	1.1	2.1	3.7	4.4	-0.4	25.5	1.4	1.4	1.0	0.8	0.7	0.7
Metal products, machinery and equipment	2.0	1.0	0.3	3.4	-2.8	9.0	4.4	4.6	5.0	4.8	4.2	4.2
Electricity, gas and water	5.5	5.8	3.0	2.7	1.6	2.3	6.0	5.6	3.2	3.2	3.5	3.5
Construction	2.4	0.0	1.8	0.1	-1.5	0.9	3.3	2.6	2.3	2.1	2.6	2.7
Traded services[1]	1.6	1.5	0.8	1.9	1.1	1.0	59.3	57.9	60.1	59.6	59.8	59.3
Non-traded services	0.3	-2.0	0.9	0.2	-1.0	0.9	12.3	14.8	15.0	16.9	17.9	18.4
Total traded goods and services	2.5	2.0	1.5	2.0	0.6	2.0	87.7	85.2	85.0	83.1	82.1	81.6

156

	1983	1984	1985	1986	1987	1988	1989	1990	1991	1992	1993	1994
C. Other indicators (current prices)												
R&D as % of GDP in manufacturing sector	4.9	5.3	5.6	5.5	5.8	5.8	6.0	6.3	6.6	6.6	..	..
Total R&D expenditure as % of total GDP	2.1	2.2	2.3	2.2	2.3	2.3	2.3	2.4	2.4	2.4	2.4	..
Government funded R&D as % of total	53.8	53.7	52.9	52.5	51.7	49.9	48.1	48.3	48.8	44.3	..	..
Breakdown of employed workforce[3] by size of establishment:												
1 to 9 employees	22.3	22.9	23.2	23.8	24.1	24.2	24.1	24.1	24.4	24.7	..	..
10 to 49 employees	26.9	27.0	27.3	27.8	28.2	28.3	28.5	28.7	28.9	29.0	..	..
50 to 199 employees	21.8	21.7	21.9	22.0	22.3	22.7	22.8	22.9	22.8	22.6	..	..
200 to 499 employees	12.5	12.3	12.1	11.9	11.6	11.7	11.8	11.7	11.6	11.6	..	..
500 employees and more	16.5	16.1	15.5	14.5	13.8	13.1	12.8	12.6	12.3	12.1	..	..
Total	100.0	100.0	100.0	100.0	100.0	100.0	100.0	100.0	100.0	100.0	..	..
Workforce (millions)	13.0	12.8	12.7	12.7	12.8	13.1	13.6	13.8	13.7	13.5	..	..

1. Wholesale and retail distribution, restaurants and hotels, transportation, warehousing and communications, finance, insurance, real estate and business services.
2. The 1980 figure is the 1980-1984 average.
3. All employees affiliated with UNEDIC (unemployment insurance scheme for private-sector employees).
Source: OECD, *National Accounts, Main Science and Technology Indicators* and OECD estimates.

157

Table H. Labour market indicators

A. Trend

	Peak	Trough	1985	1990	1992	1993	1994
Unemployment rate							
Total	1994: 12.4	1964: 1.1	10.2	8.9	10.3	11.6	12.4
Male	1994: 10.6	1965: 1.0	8.4	6.7	8.3	9.9	10.6
Female	1994: 14.7	1965: 2.5	12.7	11.7	12.9	13.8	14.7
Youth (15 to 24 years old)	1994: 27.5	1970: 3.2	25.6	19.1	20.8	24.6	27.5
Share of long-term unemployment[1]	1986: 47.8	1975: 17.0	46.8	38.0	36.1	34.2	38.3
Registered vacancies (thousands)	1973: 251.6	1993: 43.0	46.0	79.5	52.8	43.0	49.5
Length of working week[2]	1964: 45.7	1985: 38.6	38.6	38.7	38.7	38.6	..

B. Structural and institutional features

	1970	1980	1985	1990	1992	1993	1994
Labour force (% change)	1.3	0.6	0.5	0.5	0.4	0.3	1.3
Participation rate[3]							
Overall	67.6	68.4	66.4	66.6	66.8	66.7	67.4
Male	86.9	81.7	76.6	75.4	74.7	74.5	..
Female	48.5	54.4	54.8	57.6	58.8	59.0	..
Employment/population aged 15 to 64	66.0	64.1	59.6	60.7	59.8	58.9	59.0
Employers, self-employed and family workers (as % of total)	20.7	15.8	14.6	12.9	12.2	11.9	11.6
Wage earners and salaried employees (as % of total)	79.3	84.2	85.4	87.1	87.8	88.1	88.4
Civilian employment by sector (% change)							
Agriculture	-4.7	-3.8	-3.4	-4.6	-3.8	-4.4	-4.8
Industry	0.6	-1.5	-2.7	0.5	-3.5	-4.6	-2.2
Services	2.2	1.3	1.7	1.8	1.0	0.5	2.0
of which: General government	2.7	0.5	2.6	0.2	1.3	2.4	1.7
Total	0.6	-0.2	-0.1	1.1	-0.6	-1.2	0.5
Civilian employment by sector (as % of total)							
Agriculture	13.2	8.4	7.2	5.6	5.2	5.0	4.8
Industry	39.2	35.6	31.9	30.0	28.6	27.6	26.9
Services	47.6	56.0	60.9	64.4	66.2	67.4	68.4
of which: General government	18.4	20.8	23.4	23.2	23.8	24.7	25.0
Total	100.0	100.0	100.0	100.0	100.0	100.0	100.0

Temporary work[4]	..	..	0.6	1.2	1.1	0.9	..
Part-time[5]	..	..	10.8	11.8	12.7	13.9	..
Non-wage labour costs[6]	23.9	26.1	27.9	27.9	28.1	28.1	28.2
Unemployment insurance benefits[7]	..	46.9	42.0	47.6	47.0	44.8	..
Minimum wage as % of average wage	38.7	45.7	52.5	50.2	50.6	50.9	51.4

1. People looking for a job for one year or more as a percentage of total unemployment.
2. Hours worked by industrial wage-earners.
3. Labour force as a percentage of population aged 15 to 64.
4. As a percentage of dependent employment.
5. Part-time employment as a percentage of total employment (part time and full time).
6. Employer social-security contributions as a percentage of total wages.
7. Unemployment benefits per beneficiary as a percentage of average gross wage. The 1980 figure is that for 1982.

Source: OECD, Labour Force Statistics, Main Economic Indicators and OECD estimates.

159

Table I. Financial markets

	1980	1985	1989	1990	1991	1992	1993	1994
Sector size								
Sectoral employment/total employment	2.6[1]	..	2.8	2.8	2.8	2.8	..	..
Non-financial agents' financial flows/GDP[2]	..	11.5	18.8	20.6	13.1	12.1	..	..
Domestic financial assets/GDP	..	5.0	5.8	5.4	..	..	..	..
Stock-market capitalisation/GDP[3]	8.9	12.9	32.6	24.3	27.6	25.9	..	..
Density of banking network[4]	37.6	38.8	38.1	37.7	37.4	36.9	..	..
Structure of financial flows								
Share of intermediated financing in total financing[5]	72.8	58.1	54.2	59.0	46.0	18.0	..	..
Financial institutions' share of stocks of financial assets	..	49.1	35.4	37.4	36.4	36.2	..	..
Securities issues in financing flows of non-financial agents[6]	..	44.1	38.8	30.0	43.5	69.0	..	..
Structure of private non-financial sector's portfolio:[7]								
Deposits[8]	..	31.4	19.4	22.0	19.2	18.7	..	..
Money market's bonds and bills	..	4.2	3.2	3.5	3.5	3.7	..	..
Equities	..	32.0	50.2	43.1	45.5	44.3	..	..
Institutional investment[9]	..	5.2	6.5	8.0	8.4	9.1	..	..
Non-financial corporate financial structure:	..	100.0	100.0	100.0	100.0	100.0	..	..
Equity	..	45.9	64.5	56.0	57.7	57.1	..	..
Short-term debt:								
Securities	..	1.5	1.9	2.6	2.2	2.2	..	..
Other	..	30.6	19.5	23.8	23.1	22.8	..	..
Medium- and long-term debt:								
Bonds	..	4.2	2.6	3.4	3.4	3.6	..	..
Other	..	17.8	11.5	14.2	13.6	14.2	..	..
Internationalisation of markets								
Foreign business of the banking sector[10]								
Assets	32.0	39.0	36.9	30.9	30.8	31.4	..	..
Liabilities	28.9	37.6	37.4	33.8	33.4	31.4	..	..
International banking networks:								
Foreign banks in France[11]	122.0	148.0	167.0	164.0	174.0	174.0	..	..
French bank branches abroad	..	..	..	..	..	370.0	..	..
Share of cross-border transactions:								
Net purchases of foreign securities by residents	..	..	29.2	25.2	..	..	..	..
Net purchases of domestic securities by								

Cost of bank intermediation[12]	..	..	9.5	..	..	..
Interest margin[13]	2.5[1]	2.3	2.1	1.8	1.9	..
Bank productivity[14]	69.4[1]	68.5	76.3	80.8	77.3	..
Divergence between Euro-rates and domestic interest rates[15]	0.3	0.7	-0.2	-0.1	-0.1	-0.2

Indicator of market intervention

Share of preferential-rate lending in total[16]	42.8[1]	44.0	15.2	..	..	..

1. 1981 figures.
2. Net financing flows by credit institutions, UCIT's and insurance companies to non-financial institutions.
3. Shares listed.
4. Number of bank branches and head offices (excluding savings banks) per 100 000 population.
5. Definition of Conseil National du Crédit: share of financial institutions in total external financing of non-financial residents.
6. Issues of bonds, commercial papers and shares as a per cent of the net flows as defined under 2 above.
7. The private non-financial sector includes corporations as well as households and non-profit institutions. The total differs from 100 because some items are excluded.
8. National and international means of payment plus other liquid assets.
9. UCITs.
10. As a percentage of commercial banks' balance sheets (AFB banks for 1990).
11. Number of branches and subsidiaries.
12. Ratio of net banking product minus commission and fees of the member banks of the AFB and the mutual and co-operative banks.
13. Difference between interest receipts and interest payments divided by average total assets. Due to accounting changes data for 1990 have been made compatible with 1991.
14. Operating expenses divided by gross income.
15. Three-month Euro-French franc interest rate minus three-month inter bank rate.
16. New medium- and long-term loans at preferential rates (Bank of France definition) as a per cent of new credit extended.
Source: Comptes de la Nation 1992; Banque de France, *Bulletin trimestriel*; Conseil National du Crédit, *Rapport annuel 1992*.

Table J. **Public sector**

	1970	1980	1985	1990	1992	1993	1994
Budgetary indicators: general government accounts (% of GDP)							
Primary receipts (excluding interest)	37.4	43.6	46.2	45.0	45.0	45.7	46.0
Primary expenditure (excluding interest)	37.1	44.2	49.1	46.4	48.9	51.1	50.7
Primary budget balance	0.3	−0.6	−3.0	−1.4	−3.9	−5.4	−4.8
Net interest (including net capital transfers)	0.6	0.6	0.1	−0.1	−0.2	−0.7	−1.3
General-government budget balance	0.9	0.0	−2.9	−1.6	−4.0	−6.1	−6.1
of which: Central-government balance	1.0	−0.3	−2.9	−1.6	−3.0	−4.5	..
Structure of expenditure and taxes (% of GDP)							
General-government expenditure	34.2	42.3	48.8	45.8	48.7	51.5	51.0
Transfers	16.4	20.8	24.2	23.3	24.8	26.3	26.1
Subsidies	2.0	1.9	2.3	1.6	1.6	1.6	1.6
General expenditure							
Education	..	..	5.0	4.6	..	..	..
Transport	..	..	0.6	0.5	..	..	..
Health	..	..	3.2	3.1	..	..	..
Tax receipts	..	41.7	44.5	43.7	43.6	43.9	44.2
Personal income tax	..	5.4	5.7	5.2	6.0	6.1	6.2
Corporate taxes	..	2.1	2.0	2.3	1.5	1.5	1.6
Social-security contributions	..	17.8	19.3	19.3	19.4	19.6	19.3
Consumption taxes	..	12.7	13.2	12.4	11.7	11.7	12.0
of which: Value added tax	..	8.7	8.7	8.1	7.5	7.4	7.4
Other indicators							
Income tax elasticity	..	1.5	0.2	1.0	0.8	1.3	2.1
Income tax as % of total tax	..	18.1	17.3	17.2	17.2	17.4	17.7
Gross general-government debt (as % of GDP)	..	30.9	38.5	40.1	45.6	52.9	56.8
Net general-government debt (as % of GDP)	−0.8	−3.3	10.8	16.3	21.0	27.7	32.5
Tax rates (%)							
Average effective personal income tax rate	..	..	..	11.3	..	..	..
Top rate	69.8	60.0	67.0	56.8	56.8	56.8	56.8
Average marginal rate	..	..	..	19.5	..	..	..
Effective social-security contribution rate [1]	23.8	29.4	32.3	34.1	..	..	..
Standard VAT rate	17.6	17.6	18.6	18.6	18.6	18.6	18.6

1. Employer and employee contributions, plus the CSG (from 1991) as a per cent of total wage cost.
Source: OECD, *National Accounts* and *Revenue Statistics of OECD Member Countries.*

BASIC STATISTICS

BASIC STATISTICS:

INTERNATIONAL COMPARISONS

	Units	Reference period [1]	Australia	Aus...
Population				
Total	Thousands	1992	17 489	7 8
Inhabitants per sq. km	Number	1992	2	
Net average annual increase over previous 10 years	%	1992	1.4	
Employment				
Civilian employment (CE)[2]	Thousands	1992	7 637	3 5
Of which: Agriculture	% of CE		5.3	
Industry	% of CE		23.8	3
Services	% of CE		71	5
Gross domestic product (GDP)				
At current prices and current exchange rates	Bill. US$	1992	296.6	18(
Per capita	US$		16 959	23 (
At current prices using current PPPs[3]	Bill. US$	1992	294.5	)
Per capita	US$		16 800	18 (
Average annual volume growth over previous 5 years	%	1992	2	
Gross fixed capital formation (GFCF)	% of GDP	1992	19.7	
Of which: Machinery and equipment	% of GDP		9.3	
Residential construction	% of GDP		5.1	
Average annual volume growth over previous 5 years	%	1992	−1	2
Gross saving ratio[4]	% of GDP	1992	15.6	2
General government				
Current expenditure on goods and services	% of GDP	1992	18.5	1{
Current disbursements[5]	% of GDP	1992	36.9	4
Current receipts	% of GDP	1992	33.1	4{
Net official development assistance	% of GNP	1992	0.33	(
Indicators of living standards				
Private consumption per capita using current PPPs[3]	US$	1992	10 527	9 S
Passenger cars, per 1 000 inhabitants	Number	1990	430	3
Telephones, per 1 000 inhabitants	Number	1990	448	5
Television sets, per 1 000 inhabitants	Number	1989	484	4
Doctors, per 1 000 inhabitants	Number	1991	2	
Infant mortality per 1 000 live births	Number	1991	7.1	
Wages and prices (average annual increase over previous 5 years)				
Wages (earnings or rates according to availability)	%	1992	5	
Consumer prices	%	1992	5.2	
Foreign trade				
Exports of goods, fob*	Mill. US$	1992	42 844	44 3
As % of GDP	%		14.4	2
Average annual increase over previous 5 years	%		10.1	1(
Imports of goods, cif*	Mill. US$	1992	40 751	54 (
As % of GDP	%		13.7	
Average annual increase over previous 5 years	%		8.6	1(
Total official reserves[6]	Mill. SDRs	1992	8 152	9 (
As ratio of average monthly imports of goods	Ratio		2.4	

* At current prices and exchange rates.
1. Unless otherwise stated.
2. According to the definitions used in OECD *Labour Force Statistics*.
3. PPPs = Purchasing Power Parities.
4. Gross saving = Gross national disposable income minus private and government consumption.
5. Current disbursements = Current expenditure on goods and services plus current transfers and payments of property income.
6. Gold included in reserves is valued at 35 SDRs per ounce. End of year.
7. Including Luxembourg.

EMPLOYMENT OPPORTUNITIES

Economics Department, OECD

The Economics Department of the OECD offers challenging and rewarding opportunities to economists interested in applied policy analysis in an international environment. The Department's concerns extend across the entire field of economic policy analysis, both macroeconomic and microeconomic. Its main task is to provide, for discussion by committees of senior officials from Member countries, documents and papers dealing with current policy concerns. Within this programme of work, three major responsibilities are:

- to prepare regular surveys of the economies of individual Member countries;
- to issue full twice-yearly reviews of the economic situation and prospects of the OECD countries in the context of world economic trends;
- to analyse specific policy issues in a medium-term context for the OECD as a whole, and to a lesser extent for the non-OECD countries.

The documents prepared for these purposes, together with much of the Department's other economic work, appear in published form in the *OECD Economic Outlook, OECD Economic Surveys, OECD Economic Studies* and the Department's *Working Papers* series.

The Department maintains a world econometric model, INTERLINK, which plays an important role in the preparation of the policy analyses and twice-yearly projections. The availability of extensive cross-country data bases and good computer resources facilitates comparative empirical analysis, much of which is incorporated into the model.

The Department is made up of about 80 professional economists from a variety of backgrounds and Member countries. Most projects are carried out by small teams and last from four to eighteen months. Within the Department, ideas and points of view are widely discussed; there is a lively professional interchange, and all professional staff have the opportunity to contribute actively to the programme of work.

Skills the Economics Department is looking for:

a) Solid competence in using the tools of both microeconomic and macroeconomic theory to answer policy questions. Experience indicates that this normally requires the equivalent of a Ph.D. in economics or substantial relevant professional experience to compensate for a lower degree.

b) Solid knowledge of economic statistics and quantitative methods; this includes how to identify data, estimate structural relationships, apply basic techniques of time series analysis, and test hypotheses. It is essential to be able to interpret results sensibly in an economic policy context.

c) A keen interest in and extensive knowledge of policy issues, economic developments and their political/social contexts.

d) Interest and experience in analysing questions posed by policy-makers and presenting the results to them effectively and judiciously. Thus, work experience in government agencies or policy research institutions is an advantage.

e) The ability to write clearly, effectively, and to the point. The OECD is a bilingual organisation with French and English as the official languages. Candidates must have excellent knowledge of one of these languages, and some knowledge of the other. Knowledge of other languages might also be an advantage for certain posts.

f) For some posts, expertise in a particular area may be important, but a successful candidate is expected to be able to work on a broader range of topics relevant to the work of the Department. Thus, except in rare cases, the Department does not recruit narrow specialists.

g) The Department works on a tight time schedule with strict deadlines. Moreover, much of the work in the Department is carried out in small groups. Thus, the ability to work with other economists from a variety of cultural and professional backgrounds, to supervise junior staff, and to produce work on time is important.

General information

The salary for recruits depends on educational and professional background. Positions carry a basic salary from FF 305 700 or FF 377 208 for Administrators (economists) and from FF 438 348 for Principal Administrators (senior economists). This may be supplemented by expatriation and/or family allowances, depending on nationality, residence and family situation. Initial appointments are for a fixed term of two to three years.

Vacancies are open to candidates from OECD Member countries. The Organisation seeks to maintain an appropriate balance between female and male staff and among nationals from Member countries.

For further information on employment opportunities in the Economics Department, contact:

Administrative Unit
Economics Department
OECD
2, rue André-Pascal
75775 PARIS CEDEX 16
FRANCE

E-Mail: compte.esadmin@oecd.org

Applications citing "ECSUR", together with a detailed *curriculum vitae* in English or French, should be sent to the Head of Personnel at the above address.

MAIN SALES OUTLETS OF OECD PUBLICATIONS
PRINCIPAUX POINTS DE VENTE DES PUBLICATIONS DE L'OCDE

ARGENTINA – ARGENTINE
Carlos Hirsch S.R.L.
Galería Güemes, Florida 165, 4° Piso
1333 Buenos Aires   Tel. (1) 331.1787 y 331.2391
Telefax: (1) 331.1787

AUSTRALIA – AUSTRALIE
D.A. Information Services
648 Whitehorse Road, P.O.B 163
Mitcham, Victoria 3132   Tel. (03) 873.4411
Telefax: (03) 873.5679

AUSTRIA – AUTRICHE
Gerold & Co.
Graben 31
Wien I   Tel. (0222) 533.50.14
Telefax: (0222) 512.47.31.29

BELGIUM – BELGIQUE
Jean De Lannoy
Avenue du Roi 202 Koningslaan
B-1060 Bruxelles   Tel. (02) 538.51.69/538.08.41
Telefax: (02) 538.08.41

CANADA
Renouf Publishing Company Ltd.
1294 Algoma Road
Ottawa, ON K1B 3W8   Tel. (613) 741.4333
Telefax: (613) 741.5439
Stores:
61 Sparks Street
Ottawa, ON K1P 5R1   Tel. (613) 238.8985
211 Yonge Street
Toronto, ON M5B 1M4   Tel. (416) 363.3171
Telefax: (416)363.59.63
Les Éditions La Liberté Inc.
3020 Chemin Sainte-Foy
Sainte-Foy, PQ G1X 3V6   Tel. (418) 658.3763
Telefax: (418) 658.3763
Federal Publications Inc.
165 University Avenue, Suite 701
Toronto, ON M5H 3B8   Tel. (416) 860.1611
Telefax: (416) 860.1608
Les Publications Fédérales
1185 Université
Montréal, QC H3B 3A7   Tel. (514) 954.1633
Telefax: (514) 954.1635

CHINA – CHINE
China National Publications Import
Export Corporation (CNPIEC)
16 Gongti E. Road, Chaoyang District
P.O. Box 88 or 50
Beijing 100704 PR   Tel. (01) 506.6688
Telefax: (01) 506.3101

CHINESE TAIPEI – TAIPEI CHINOIS
Good Faith Worldwide Int'l. Co. Ltd.
9th Floor, No. 118, Sec. 2
Chung Hsiao E. Road
Taipei   Tel. (02) 391.7396/391.7397
Telefax: (02) 394.9176

**CZECH REPUBLIC – RÉPUBLIQUE
TCHÈQUE**
Artia Pegas Press Ltd.
Narodni Trida 25
POB 825
111 21 Praha 1   Tel. 26.65.68
Telefax: 26.20.81

DENMARK – DANEMARK
Munksgaard Book and Subscription Service
35, Nørre Søgade, P.O. Box 2148
DK-1016 København K   Tel. (33) 12.85.70
Telefax: (33) 12.93.87

EGYPT – ÉGYPTE
Middle East Observer
41 Sherif Street
Cairo   Tel. 392.6919
Telefax: 360-6804

FINLAND – FINLANDE
Akateeminen Kirjakauppa
Keskuskatu 1, P.O. Box 128
00100 Helsinki
Subscription Services/Agence d'abonnements :
P.O. Box 23
00371 Helsinki   Tel. (358 0) 121 4416
Telefax: (358 0) 121.4450

FRANCE
OECD/OCDE
Mail Orders/Commandes par correspondance:
2, rue André-Pascal
75775 Paris Cedex 16   Tel. (33-1) 45.24.82.00
Telefax: (33-1) 49.10.42.76
Telex: 640048 OCDE
Internet: Compte.PUBSINQ @ oecd.org
Orders via Minitel, France only/
Commandes par Minitel, France exclusivement :
36 15 OCDE
OECD Bookshop/Librairie de l'OCDE :
33, rue Octave-Feuillet
75016 Paris   Tel. (33-1) 45.24.81.81
(33-1) 45.24.81.67
Documentation Française
29, quai Voltaire
75007 Paris   Tel. 40.15.70.00
Gibert Jeune (Droit-Économie)
6, place Saint-Michel
75006 Paris   Tel. 43.25.91.19
Librairie du Commerce International
10, avenue d'Iéna
75016 Paris   Tel. 40.73.34.60
Librairie Dunod
Université Paris-Dauphine
Place du Maréchal de Lattre de Tassigny
75016 Paris   Tel. (1) 44.05.40.13
Librairie Lavoisier
11, rue Lavoisier
75008 Paris   Tel. 42.65.39.95
Librairie L.G.D.J. - Montchrestien
20, rue Soufflot
75005 Paris   Tel. 46.33.89.85
Librairie des Sciences Politiques
30, rue Saint-Guillaume
75007 Paris   Tel. 45.48.36.02
P.U.F.
49, boulevard Saint-Michel
75005 Paris   Tel. 43.25.83.40
Librairie de l'Université
12a, rue Nazareth
13100 Aix-en-Provence   Tel. (16) 42.26.18.08
Documentation Française
165, rue Garibaldi
69003 Lyon   Tel. (16) 78.63.32.23
Librairie Decitre
29, place Bellecour
69002 Lyon   Tel. (16) 72.40.54.54
Librairie Sauramps
Le Triangle
34967 Montpellier Cedex 2   Tel. (16) 67.58.85.15
Telefax: (16) 67.58.27.36

GERMANY – ALLEMAGNE
OECD Publications and Information Centre
August-Bebel-Allee 6
D-53175 Bonn   Tel. (0228) 959.120
Telefax: (0228) 959.12.17

GREECE – GRÈCE
Librairie Kauffmann
Mavrokordatou 9
106 78 Athens   Tel. (01) 32.55.321
Telefax: (01) 32.30.320

HONG-KONG
Swindon Book Co. Ltd.
Astoria Bldg. 3F
34 Ashley Road, Tsimshatsui
Kowloon, Hong Kong   Tel. 2376.2062
Telefax: 2376.0685

HUNGARY – HONGRIE
Euro Info Service
Margitsziget, Európa Ház
1138 Budapest   Tel. (1) 111.62.16
Telefax: (1) 111.60.61

ICELAND – ISLANDE
Mál Mog Menning
Laugavegi 18, Pósthólf 392
121 Reykjavik   Tel. (1) 552.4240
Telefax: (1) 562.3523

INDIA – INDE
Oxford Book and Stationery Co.
Scindia House
New Delhi 110001   Tel. (11) 331.5896/5308
Telefax: (11) 332.5993
17 Park Street
Calcutta 700016   Tel. 240832

INDONESIA – INDONÉSIE
Pdii-Lipi
P.O. Box 4298
Jakarta 12042   Tel. (21) 573.34.67
Telefax: (21) 573.34.67

IRELAND – IRLANDE
Government Supplies Agency
Publications Section
4/5 Harcourt Road
Dublin 2   Tel. 661.31.11
Telefax: 475.27.60

ISRAEL
Praedicta
5 Shatner Street
P.O. Box 34030
Jerusalem 91430   Tel. (2) 52.84.90/1/2
Telefax: (2) 52.84.93
R.O.Y. International
P.O. Box 13056
Tel Aviv 61130   Tel. (3) 546 1423
Telefax: (3) 546 1442
Palestinian Authority/Middle East:
INDEX Information Services
P.O.B. 19502
Jerusalem   Tel. (2) 27.12.19
Telefax: (2) 27.16.34

ITALY – ITALIE
Libreria Commissionaria Sansoni
Via Duca di Calabria 1/1
50125 Firenze   Tel. (055) 64.54.15
Telefax: (055) 64.12.57
Via Bartolini 29
20155 Milano   Tel. (02) 36.50.83
Editrice e Libreria Herder
Piazza Montecitorio 120
00186 Roma   Tel. 679.46.28
Telefax: 678.47.51
Libreria Hoepli
Via Hoepli 5
20121 Milano   Tel. (02) 86.54.46
Telefax: (02) 805.28.86
Libreria Scientifica
Dott. Lucio de Biasio 'Aeiou'
Via Coronelli, 6
20146 Milano   Tel. (02) 48.95.45.52
Telefax: (02) 48.95.45.48

JAPAN – JAPON
OECD Publications and Information Centre
Landic Akasaka Building
2-3-4 Akasaka, Minato-ku
Tokyo 107   Tel. (81.3) 3586.2016
Telefax: (81.3) 3584.7929

KOREA – CORÉE
Kyobo Book Centre Co. Ltd.
P.O. Box 1658, Kwang Hwa Moon
Seoul   Tel. 730.78.91
Telefax: 735.00.30

PRINTED IN FRANCE

•

OECD PUBLICATIONS
2, rue André-Pascal
75775 PARIS CEDEX 16
No. 48209
(10 95 14 1) ISBN 92-64-14588-5
ISSN 0376-6438

•